FROM HAUGHTY TO HUMBLE

THE LIFE OF MOSES

M.J. FERGUSON

ISBN 978-1-63814-000-9 (Paperback)
ISBN 978-1-63814-001-6 (Digital)

Copyright © 2021 M.J. Ferguson
All rights reserved
First Edition

All rights reserved. No part of this publication may be reproduced, distributed, or transmitted in any form or by any means, including photocopying, recording, or other electronic or mechanical methods without the prior written permission of the publisher. For permission requests, solicit the publisher via the address below.

Covenant Books, Inc.
11661 Hwy 707
Murrells Inlet, SC 29576
www.covenantbooks.com

CONTENTS

Prologue 5

1. Israelite History 7
2. Hebrew Baby Rescued 11
3. Boy Moses 15
4. Early Palace Days 18
5. Royal Education 21
6. The Abdication 25
7. The Mud Pits/The Murder 30
8. Fugitive to Midian 33
9. History Revealed/Proposal to Zipporah 38
10. The Burning Bush 43
11. Return to Egypt 46
12. Thutmose III 49
    Uraeus, the Cobra God 55
    The First Plague: Blood 57
    The Second Plague: Frogs 59
    The Third Plague: Fleas/Lice 61
    The Fourth Plague: Swarms 63
    The Fifth Plague: Livestock Death 67
    The Sixth Plague: Boils 69
    The Seventh Plague: Hail 71
    The Eighth Plague: Locust 73
    The Ninth Plague: Darkness 77
    The Tenth Plague: Death Pronouncement 79

13.	Death of Firstborn	80
14.	The Exodus	83
15.	The Red Sea	85
16.	Bitter Waters/Manna Begins	88
17.	Water from the Rock	92
18.	Jethro's Advice	95
19.	Mount Sinai/Ten Commandments Spoken	97
20.	The Golden Calf/Commandments Broken	99
21.	The Tabernacle/Commandments Written	104
22.	Miriam's Rebellion	108
23.	The Twelve Spies at Canaan	111
24.	Korah's Rebellion/Death of Miriam	114
25.	The Sin of Moses	117
26.	The Death of Aaron	119
27.	Venomous Snakes/Balaam's Curse	121
28.	The Death of Moses	123

Epilogue 127

PROLOGUE

Born to Hebrew slave parents, Moses was destined to toil and die as one himself. But strange circumstances changed the life of this baby, who was found in a basket floating on the Nile River by Hatshepsut, the Princess of Egypt. This teenage princess desired to adopt this baby as her own son. Being young and inexperienced, the princess gave permission to a Hebrew woman to raise her son, Moses, until he was old enough to move to the palace.

At twelve years of age, Moses was brought to his new residence. As the son of the princess, he was raised and educated to be the next Pharaoh. The Prince of Egypt was the pride of his adopted mother and all of Egypt.

Many years later, and upon seeing the living conditions and the cruel servitude of his people, the Israelites, Moses remembered the words of his Hebrew mother, Jochebed, that he was destined by Yahweh to return His people to the promised land of Canaan. After abdicating his right to the throne of Egypt, Moses determined to free his people by using his military knowledge and skill. But his own people didn't trust him, and after killing an Egyptian in hate, he was forced to flee Egypt. With a price on his head by Pharaoh Thutmose II, Moses spent the next forty years in Midian of Arabia, herding sheep until God, the Great I AM, called him to return to Egypt.

The plea of "Let My people go" was ignored by Pharaoh Thutmose III. Ten devastating plagues were brought upon the Egyptians, proving their gods to be worthless. After Pharaoh's oldest son was killed by the final plague, the king of Egypt demanded the Israelites to "leave this very night."

Before entering into the promised land of Canaan, the Israelites saw many evidences of the power and protection of God—the Great I AM. They experienced the crossing of the Red Sea and witnessed the Egyptian Army destroyed. They were given daily manna and drinking water for themselves and their herds and received the Ten Commandments spoken by God. They saw continual evidence of His presence in the cloud by day and the pillar of fire by night.

According to the Jewish timelines, the date of the Exodus was 1446 BC of the eighteenth Egyptian dynasty. The Pharaoh, at this time, was Thutmose III and not Rameses the Great of the nineteenth dynasty as is commonly believed and portrayed.

This book begins with a brief history of Moses' ancestors, the Israelites, and the events leading to their servitude and slavery by the king of Egypt, Pharaoh Amenhotep I, who "knew not Joseph."

M.J. FERGUSON

This is the history of Moses's life of 120 years from his birth in Egypt to his death on Mount Nebo overlooking the Jordan River into the promised land. Moses was buried by the angels in the valley of Moab until his resurrection by God.

Many scenes and conversations in this book are added to better portray and represent events, but in no area is it *contradictory* to the Holy Bible.

CHAPTER 1

ISRAELITE HISTORY

The history of my ancestors began when Jacob, the son of Isaac, was given the new name of "Israel" by the angel of God at the river, Jabbok. Therefore, all of his twelve sons and their families were called Israelites. Living in Canaan, they had bountiful fields of wheat and many herds of sheep. Their families and servants were healthy, strong, prosperous, and blessed of God.

The twelve brothers were sons of four different women—two wives and two concubines of Jacob. The two youngest sons, however, were by his favorite wife, Rachel. There was conflict and hostility between the brothers, but they shared their mutual resentfulness toward their father's favored son, Joseph. During a fit of rage and jealousy, ten of the older brothers sold their younger brother, the eleventh son of Jacob, to some merchants traveling to Egypt for twenty pieces of silver—the price of a slave. To cover their treacherous act, they smeared blood on his grand and colorful coat (a gift from Jacob; an indication of Joseph's status as the "favorite") and told their father that some animal had probably killed the young man.

With a broken heart, Joseph traveled in chains to Egypt to be sold and, in all likelihood, perish as a slave. Through the grace of God, he did not die but was blessed. He became a trusted servant in the household of Potiphar, the captain of Pharaoh's guard.

After years of loyal service to Potiphar, Joseph was condemned to prison by means of false accusations made by Potiphar's wife. Eventually, after Joseph had been in prison for several years, he was given the opportunity to interpret Pharaoh's troublesome dream of an impending and severe famine throughout all the land of Egypt and other nations.

By the grace of God, and the king of Egypt, Joseph became the Vizier of Egypt at age thirty. He was second only to Pharaoh himself. In addition to this high honor and position, Joseph was given a wife and a new name, Zaphenath-Paaneah, which is interpreted as "savior of the world."

Zaphenath-Paaneah (Joseph) made the king of Egypt very rich by increasing his lands, storing the grain produced by the seven years of plenty, and selling the grain during the seven years of drought as foretold by God to Pharaoh in a dream. People from all surrounding nations came to Egypt to buy the plentiful grain.

During the severe drought, Jacob, the father of our nation, sent ten of his sons to Egypt to buy grain. It was during their second travel to buy more grain, that Joseph revealed himself to his brothers.

With the permission and blessing of Pharaoh, Joseph sent for his father and all his descendants to move to Egypt where there was plenty of food. In appreciation for Joseph's work and service, Pharaoh gave them the land of Goshen.

Goshen is in the northern territory of lower Egypt, where the Nile River flows north and splits into many rivers and streams. It was the ideal land for crops, sheep, and other livestock, and for a while, the Israelites were exempt from paying taxes. Egyptians abhorred and despised shepherds, but Pharaoh acknowledged that Joseph's God had blessed Egypt and other surrounding nations from starving due to the drought and famine. Through the powerful protection of Joseph and the grace of God, my ancestors, the Israelites, prospered and grew strong.

Joseph had two sons, Manasseh and Ephraim. Before Joseph died, he earnestly requested that his bones be taken to Canaan when his family would leave Egypt and return to the land promised to Abraham, Isaac, and Jacob. He died at 110 years of age and was embalmed and buried as was the Egyptian practice for royalty or honored status.

Many years later, Amenhotep I became the second Egyptian Pharaoh of the eighteenth dynasty. When he and his entourage of royal chariots took an extensive tour of the country and "his" nation, he came upon the rich and fertile land of northern Egypt, where the Nile River supplied ample water for crops and livestock. It was obviously inhabited by "foreigners" and disgusting shepherds! They didn't dress like Egyptians, nor did they speak the language of the Egyptian nation.

Weeks later and upon returning to his palace, Pharaoh called for the scribes.

"Look into the history of those foreigners in Goshen. Who are they? Where did they come from? Why do they occupy such a large and fertile area of Egypt?"

With his eyes cast downward, the spokesman of the scribes said, "Oh mighty Pharaoh, Son of Ra, and god incarnate, god of the heavens and the earth, we have discovered the history of those people in Goshen of lower Egypt that you have inquired about."

"Yes, yes, yes. What is it?"

"About three hundred years ago, your predecessor gave this land to the family members of his vizier, Zaphenath-Paaneah, as a gift for saving Egypt and the surrounding nations from starving during a severe seven-year drought."

"Zaphenath-Paaneah? Hmm, doesn't that name mean 'savior of the world'?"

"Yes, Sire."

"Never heard of him!"

"There is one more thing, oh Son of Ra. Please forgive us, but there is no record of these people ever paying any taxes."

"What? No taxes? They are living on a great and fertile land provided for them by Hapi, the god of the Nile? And they are not paying any tax?"

"No, Sire. We mean, yes, Sire. You are correct, Sire. They pay no taxes to you, Sire."

"That will stop *now*! Everyone in Egypt pays taxes, and they are no exception! Tax them! And tax them heavily! Make up for those lost years!"

That command by Amenhotep I, the Pharaoh of Egypt, was the beginning of the oppression toward my people in Goshen. Up until then, the Israelites lived in relative peace and comfort, growing in number, strength, and wealth. Then taxes came! Still the Israelites prospered!

Even though a great increase of revenue came to the Pharaoh with the taxation of the Israelites, Amenhotep I became fearful of the Hebrew prosperity and growing numbers.

While pacing back and forth on his palace balcony and looking north toward the distant area of Goshen, he said to his advice councilors, "What are we to do with those increasing foreigners, called Israelites, in the north? I fear they may be of greater number than we are. When we go to war with other nations, might these foreigners on *our* land, rebel and join their strength with our enemies to fight against us especially now that they are being heavily taxed? Let us deal shrewdly with these people."

"Oh Great Pharaoh, when we war with other nations, we do not kill all their strong men. We bring the best men and women here to make slaves for us. Our slaves help make Egypt rich and powerful. Let us do the same with those Hebrews. They can work for us! They can build for us. Let us now make slaves of those foreigners in Goshen."

"Yes, yes. Your idea has merit. I like it. If we make slaves of them, their numbers and strength will diminish. We will weaken their spirits *and* their backs by demanding an oppressive workload on this ever-growing population."

Thus, many thousands of Israelites were rounded up and forced to live in slave quarters up and down the Nile and near the capital city of Thebes.

Subsequently, on top of heavy taxation and forced servitude, much of the Israelites' possessions were confiscated, and numerous homes were destroyed or burned. They were forced to build small cottages of mud bricks and thatched roofs as "adequate shelter" for their families. But much of the work energy was assigned to building the storage cities of Pithom and Rameses in Goshen. Still, with the blessings of God, the Hebrews continued to prosper.

Later, because of the continued strength and prosperity of the enslaved Israelites, Pharaoh ordered a couple of Hebrew midwives to kill all the newborn male babies. But the midwives were God-fearing women and did not carry out the king's command.

When they were summoned before Pharaoh and questioned by him, they respectfully said, "Oh mighty Pharaoh, Hebrew women are not like Egyptian women. They are strong and independent, and we are denied the opportunity to assist during the birthing of their babies."

This, of course, was a lie, but God blessed these midwives and made them prosper.

All of the Israelites were blessed and continued to grow in strength and numbers, which feared and angered Pharaoh Amenhotep I.

*****

I was born into a slave family and therefore destined to live and die as a bondsman in Egypt. My future was fated to be the same as my recent predecessors—live as a slave and die as one in Egypt.

Shortly before I was born to Amram and Jochebed, Pharaoh Amenhotep ordered a new and severely barbaric decree, "Every new son born to the Hebrews shall be killed by any means and cast into the Nile. They are too many in number and becoming increasingly too mighty for us."

Violence ensued, and screaming was heard throughout all of Goshen as Egyptian soldiers searched every house for male babies. Coldly and savagely, they ripped the newborn sons from their mothers' arms.

"No! Please don't take my baby! Please! Please! *Please!*"

Without apparent feeling or concern for the screaming parents, the Egyptian soldiers viciously snatched the crying babies from loving arms—arms not strong enough to resist and arms not strong enough to protect their newborns, whose only crime was being born "male." These innocent boy babies, whether instantly killed or left alive, were viciously thrown into the Nile River to drown or to be fed to the crocodiles! It was a fearsome and devastating stage in our history. It was worse than the heavy taxation, worse than the slavery, and worse than the taskmaster's whip.

Pregnant with me and nearing delivery time, my mother cried desperately.

"Oh, God, You have promised to return our people to Canaan, the land of our ancestors, but we are now in bondage to Egypt, and cruelty has increased! How can I protect my child, if it is a male, from Pharaoh's decree? Please give me strength and wisdom to know your will."

After I was born and for the next three months, I was carefully hidden from the Egyptian soldiers—and from the other mothers whose babies had been ripped from their arms and murdered. In their anger and jealousy and in hopes of receiving special privileges or gifts, some Hebrew women reported to the Egyptian soldiers their knowledge of newborn males. Hebrews against Hebrews! Mothers against mothers! Deplorable, and inexcusable. All because of their own pain and resentment for losing their sons. Suspicion and mistrust permeated the homes and streets.

Keeping me hidden and quiet from the Egyptian soldiers and *spies* was becoming more and more difficult in our small house. Finally, unable to continue with her secret any longer, my mother and sister devised a plan. They quietly collected reeds and wove a basket with a hinged covering. They made it waterproof with pitch and tar. With tears running down her face and wondering if she would ever see me again, my mother placed me in this little ark and closed the lid.

Then in the predawn light, she and my sister, Miriam, carried me to the Nile River and carefully situated the basket among the tall reeds close to the edge.

With a weak and fragile faith in God, my mother urged, "Miriam, watch over your baby brother. There is nothing more we can do. He is in God's hands now. If Yahweh has a plan for him, he will be saved!"

CHAPTER 2

HEBREW BABY RESCUED

The royal princess, Hatshepsut, and her entourage of young maids came to bathe at the edge of the water while several Egyptian guards with spears and swords stood sentry for their protection. Like graceful swans at the river's edge, they were thoroughly enjoying the cool and refreshing water in the hot Egyptian sun, laughing, squealing, and splashing each other.

Suddenly, one maiden said, "Look, Princess, there is a basket floating among the reeds. Shall I get it for you?"

After a quick look toward her protectors, she said, "Yes, of course, but be careful. Crocodiles!"

Upon opening the lid to the basket, the sun hit my eyes, and I began to cry. Looking at me and the Hebrew blanket I was wrapped in, the princess said, "Look, it's a *baby! A baby boy!* Obviously, a *Hebrew*."

She quickly positioned the basket to keep the sun off my face.

"Look at him! He is so beautiful! Some mother is clearly trying to save his life from the command of the king to kill all Hebrew male babies."

Then quietly, to herself and to those only very close to her, she said, "I will keep him and raise this baby as my own son. After all, what can only *one* Hebrew male baby to do hurt Pharaoh's dynasty?"

Then she added, "Since *I* saved him and drew him out of the water, *I* get to name him. So I must choose a royal Egyptian name. Hmm…my mother's name is Ahmose, and my father's name is Thutmose, sometimes called Thutmoses, and soon to be the next Pharaoh of Egypt, so I will name this beautiful boy *Moses*! He will be *my* son and an Egyptian! And he will be the Prince of Egypt!"

"My princess, the gods are truly smiling on you, and honoring you with a gift. A gift of a beautiful baby for your very own, but how will you feed him?" one of her older maidens questioned.

At that query, the younger maidens hushed their giggling and searched the princess's face for her response.

"Perhaps someone in the royal harem can…"

Just then, my sister, who had been watching and hiding among the tall grass by the river's edge, walked bravely but cautiously toward the young princess. The Egyptian guards apparently did not think my sister was a threat to the young princess and let her approach.

"Oh, Princess! It looks like you have found a baby. Was it in a basket floating on the river? May I take a little peek at the baby?"

Not looking up at Miriam but smiling at the baby now cradled tenderly in her royal arms, the princess gave a little nod. Surprised by my sister's boldness and the permission given to her, the young maidens backed away.

"Oh, Princess, this is a *male* baby and wrapped in *Hebrew* cloth! He must have been hidden here to save his life."

"Yes. Isn't he the sweetest thing? Look, he is holding onto my finger."

Cautiously, my sister added, "Oh, Princess, he is smiling at you too. He seems to like you! You must be very kind." Then she carefully said, "Your Highness, if you don't already have plans on how you are to care for such a young baby, perhaps I can find a woman…a Hebrew woman who is willing to nurse the baby for you."

With a nod from the princess, Miriam ran home to get our mother, Jochebed.

Being out of breath from running so fast, Miriam finally was able to tell what had happened.

"Mother, Mother, the princess and her maidens found our baby…my baby brother. The princess needs someone to nurse him for her. Come quickly! Perhaps she will let us bring him to *our* home."

Upon arrival at the river where the royal princess was still holding me close to herself, my mother and sister bowed low and respectfully before being announced by one of the maidens.

"Your Highness."

The princess looked up and said, "Come. I am going to adopt this beautiful baby as *my own*. He is *mine!* Do you understand?" Without waiting for a response from my mother, she continued, "Are you willing to nurse him and care for him until he is old enough to come to the palace as *my son?*"

Bowing low, my mother said, as calmly as she could as to not show her emotions, "Yes, your Highness, I am willing. I will do all that you request of me."

"Fine. I will pay you wages, and you will have protection for yourself and my baby…*my son!* Surely, the king's decree to kill Hebrew male babies cannot last much longer and especially if this baby belongs to *me!* By the way, his name is 'Moses,' the name *I* have given to him, which is a royal *Egyptian* name. Do you understand?"

Even though my mother understood and spoke only a little of the Egyptian language, she understood the substance of the message and was thrilled for the opportunity to take her son home—at least for a brief while.

I was born from the line of Levi, the third son of Jacob by Leah. All of this history was told to me as I grew older. But my earliest memories of my childhood were those of being cherished by my real mother and family. I learned about our heritage and the God of our fathers.

My family lived in a simple small mud brick home with minimal furnishings in the slave quarters not far from the capital city of Thebes. The table and chairs all teetered, and our beds were boxed frames filled with straw. The fireplace was small and used mostly for cooking. A few dented pots hung from wooden pegs, and our precious water jug was in the corner. Cozy was a word that gave a picture of warmth and comfort, but in our case, "cozy" meant tight and confined surroundings, yet that was all I would know for the first twelve years of my life. It was, after all, "my home."

When I was about four or five years old, I was told, "Moses, you have been adopted by the king's daughter, and when you are old enough, you will go and live in the palace with her as *her son, the Prince of Egypt.*"

With wide eyes, I didn't understand what all that meant, and I didn't like the thought of leaving my home and family. But over and over, she told me the story of how my life was saved by God and that God had a special plan for me.

She added, "God promised our father, Jacob, that He would have us return to Canaan, and I believe that you, Moses, are the person God has chosen to lead us out of Egypt and our bondage. You must grow up strong and true to God's plan for your life."

Since our people were in bondage to the Egyptian Pharaoh, everyone was forced to work hard for this cruel king. My father and sister were gone during the day working, but my mother was allowed to stay home with me and my brother, Aaron, who was only three years older than me. The princess sent money to my mother for my extra food and care. (I didn't know her name until I moved to the palace.)

A few times during my youth, the royal princess with her entourage of maidens and guards stopped by our humble home to see me. Following my mother's example, we both bowed to the princess. She always brought a strange-looking small statue and spoke kindly to me in a language I didn't understand. But mostly, it was an Egyptian officer who frequently checked on my health and development. He would scrutinize my teeth, eyes, and ears, and he always measured my height. He was tall, very tanned, shaved head, and wore black lines around his fierce eyes. He never smiled. Then just before leaving our home, he would hand my mother her stipend in a small leather pouch along with a basket of fruit and bread.

The time was getting near for me to leave the only loving home I knew. I dreaded the thought of going to the palace with the fierce-looking soldiers and often said I didn't want to go.

"Mother, please. I don't want to leave. I am afraid. Please keep me here with you!"

My mother would wrap her arms around me and smile weakly. In a voice that sounded choked with emotion, she would say, "God will take care of you, my son. You must be true and faithful to Yahweh. Always remember that God has a plan for your life." She also warned, "The palace of Pharaoh has many riches and strange gods, and numerous temptations will surround you continually. Always know that I and your family will be praying daily for you and your safety." She added sadly, "Another thing, Moses, the royal princess is your *adoptive* mother. Don't ever say to her that you *know* that we are your *real* family. No one must ever know! For everyone's safety, you must always accept her as your mother."

Strange gods and temptations? My mother didn't know the half of it!

Baby Moses

CHAPTER 3

BOY MOSES

At the unknown appointed time when I was twelve years old, a company of Egyptian soldiers arrived at our humble home. Without knocking on our door, two armed soldiers and three other men entered our cottage. My mother instantly grabbed me for protection. But what could one small woman do in the face of these men with such strength and authority? We were as powerless as newborn lambs. The tall soldier seized my mother's trembling body and pulled her to a corner of the room while another man wrenched me from her arms.

What is happening to me? What is happening to my mother?

The second soldier stood in front of the open door, and the window shutters were flung open to let in more light. The horses outside, which occasionally whinnied and stomped their hooves, were surrounded by armed soldiers. Two horses stood in front of a royal-looking chariot, while other horses pulled a couple of carts behind. The whole entourage overwhelmed the narrow lane in front of our house, preventing onlookers from seeing what was happening. Not that anyone would *dare* to look or question the activity!

An olive-skinned man, shaved head and dressed in a white flowing robe, stood off to the side. He barked orders to the men who were bare chested and wore white, knee-length wrappings. He spoke fast cryptic words I didn't understand. It was difficult to determine his age because of his shaved head and heavy black lines around his eyes, but he had deep creases to both cheeks. His hands were smooth with dark spots on the tops. His wrists, and arms above his elbows, had gold bands. His shoes had pointed toes that curled back over the tops of his feet and tied around his ankles.

The language I spoke was, naturally, Hebrew, but I understood a few words of this strange Egyptian tongue. My mother taught me what she knew but had limited knowledge of this language or skill in its communication. It really wasn't enough to understand their rapid-fire exchange.

With fear in my mother's eyes, she nodded to me saying, "Moses, keep quiet and cooperate with these men. They are not here to hurt you!"

After ripping my clothes off and throwing them into the fireplace used for cooking and heat, they began to cut my hair. I was afraid they would shave my head to look like those men who were surrounding me, but they didn't. My hair was not shaved—just cut very short. I kept looking to my mother for reassurance, who was still in the grasp of the formidable Egyptian. All she could do was to smile slightly and nod—indicating that everything was all right.

After that, they had me stand in a large basin of water while two men gave me a bath, head to toe with warm, sudsy, and sweet-smelling water. As frightening as this was, I must say that while they worked fast, I was treated with gentleness—unless I tried to resist. *Resistance was not possible. Out of the question!*

With a nod and apparent approval from the Egyptian in charge, a large basket of new clothes was opened in front of me. Such fancy and rich-looking clothes I had never seen before. They even felt heavy on my small body. *This was kind of fun.* Then I looked at my mother, and her tattered old slave clothes. I felt sad and embarrassed, not embarrassed for *her* but embarrassed for the way *I* looked. These royal robes did not belong on the son of the slave woman standing in the corner with the intimidating Egyptian beside her.

After all the preparations were finished, which probably took less than an hour, my captors were ready to take me to the Egyptian palace. Bowing to the Egyptian in the flowing white robes, my mother respectfully and timidly asked if she could accompany me to the palace and present me to my Egyptian mother, Princess Hatshepsut. With a slight nod and a wave of his ringed fingers, my mother was reluctantly allowed to accompany me to the palace. *Accompany?* Yes, but she was not allowed to ride in the same carriage with me. She rode in the last wagon with the empty water basin and other articles of their mission.

I had often seen Egyptian chariots stop in front of our cottage. They were always impressive with two large wheels, gold trim, and emblems of one or more of their gods on the sides or front. However, the chariot carrying Princess Hatshepsut, my adoptive Egyptian mother, was much larger, more elaborate, and royal looking with an ornate chair and a fringed canopy to protect her from the blazing sun. Her carriage had four wheels, four matched horses, a driver, and room for three maidens to assist her. Of course, there were always two or more armed soldiers on horseback to guard this royal princess.

I never imagined I would ever ride in a chariot, but here I was being lifted onto this one and shown where to "hold on tight" while one of the guards stood close to me with his hand on my back. I tried to look for my mother, but she was sitting on the floor of the third carriage, among the water jugs and baskets.

All I could think of was "wind"—wind I had never experienced before. Wind in my short hair, wind making my new clothes wave and flap, and wind in the horses' manes keeping step and rhythm with their running. Such speed! Was this Egyptian driver in a hurry to get to the palace or in a hurry to leave the slave community? I didn't know where I was going or what to expect. But I did realize my confined and protected way of life was about to change.

FROM HAUGHTY TO HUMBLE

Boy Moses

CHAPTER 4

EARLY PALACE DAYS

Shortly before being taken to the palace as the royal son of Hatshepsut, the cruel king, Pharaoh Amenhotep, died, making Thutmose I the succeeding Pharaoh and sun god. He was Hatshepsut's father and therefore my adoptive grandfather. He was distant toward me, but I felt he was tolerant for the sake of his daughter. During his reign, he had many campaigns for gaining lands, power, and slaves. All for the glory of Egypt.

After arriving at the palace, I was presented to the royal princess, Hatshepsut, by the Egyptian in the white flowing robes, while my mother stood about ten paces behind me. This woman was dressed in very sheer, gauzy material of white and pale blue, trimmed in gold. She wore several gold bracelets on her wrists and arms and many rings on her fingers—and even her toes! Her hair was jet black and shoulder length, and she wore a gold headband. I recognized her as the same woman who came to see me a few times in my earlier youth.

This woman is my adoptive mother. Excuse me—my mother.

At my "presentation," I was told where to stand in front of this impressive and important-looking woman, who was surrounded by other women of less spectacular adornments. She was not very tall but filled the room with her existence. She did not smile but nodded and seemed pleased with my appearance—from head to toe!

She walked slowly to me, touched my cheek and clean short hair, and said with a slight bow, "Moses, my son, Moses, the Prince of Egypt. Welcome!"

Then she handed me a gift—a small golden image of an Egyptian god. Which god it was, I didn't know. Some of their idol gods had bodies of humans with heads of animals—ugly and frightening.

I don't know what our God looks like, but I am certain He doesn't look like one of these hideous idols.

I was permitted to give only a short "goodbye wave" to my mother before I was whisked off to a large apartment with lots of women and children. A hush fell over the room as all eyes were fixed on me. The Egyptian in the long, white robe spoke something I didn't understand, and immediately, everyone stood and said my name.

"Moses! Moses! Moses!"

Later, I learned this was the royal harem where I would spend most of my early days in the palace. I had so much to learn about my new life—and new language!

Being the son of Hatshepsut, and the "Prince of Egypt," I was given a special bedroom of my own that I did *not* like. It was larger than the whole house of my Hebrew parents.

When I saw the massive bed, I wondered, *How many will be sharing this bed with me?*

But it was only for me—*alone!* Alone and lonely! Except I was never really *alone;* someone was always in attendance watching over me.

I longed to be back home in my own bed that I shared with my brother, Aaron. Since our cottage was so small, and to make our living space larger, we always lifted our box frame beds in the morning to lean against a wall. Our floor was dirt but covered with straw, which was neither cold nor hot to our feet but soft and comforting. Sometimes, new straw would be put down making it smell sweet and fresh.

The floor of this large bedroom was hard and cold marble. The windows in my new room had gauzy, white curtains that moved in the warm breeze. Hanging from the ceiling was a canopy of sheer material that surrounded my bed.

When I asked my overseer what it was, he just laughed and said, "It is to protect Your Highness from insects while you sleep."

There is so much for me to learn!

Everything was strange to me—the language, the lessons, the clothes, the food, the music, the worship of the sun, and their *many strange gods*. I was told if the gods were pleased with me, I would receive protection and many blessings. I was also warned that some of their gods were cruel and needed to be feared! Many looked menacing to me!

How can these gods made of stone or wood possibly be helpful or even dangerous?

While living in the slave quarters with my parents and ancestors, I was afraid of the Egyptian soldiers and their cruelty. But here in the palace, the attendants were considerate and helpful to me. I was given many special privileges and was treated as *royalty*. Well, I guess I *was* royalty—now. I was the adopted son of Princess Hatshepsut and a prince in line to the throne of Egypt.

How can this be? The son of Hebrew slaves, a king, Pharaoh of Egypt.

I was totally overwhelmed by the beautiful palace with all its gold, shining marble, ivory, jewels, plush fabrics of all colors and textures, and fans made of bird feathers. I was given strict instructions on how to present myself before the Pharaoh. The Egyptians considered Pharaoh to be a god and that he was a direct descendant of Ra, the sun god, which made him also a "sun god."

"Moses, as you don't ever look directly at the sun in the sky, don't ever look directly into the eyes of the king…unless he invites you to."

My Egyptian mother was stunning and very young—*much* younger than my Hebrew mother. She wore heavy black lines around her eyes. Her hair was thick, black, and in tiny braids with beads. She wore lots of gold bracelets and jeweled necklaces. Her clothes were shear and flowed when she walked or with the slightest breeze.

To my young mind, I thought to myself, *It must take her forever to get dressed in the morning.*

I didn't see her very often because most of my care was given by the women of the royal harem. When she came to see me, she always brought me a small gift as a token of her "love." She was always kind and generous to me, but I never felt any true attachment or warmth from her. She would run a finger down the side of my face and lift my chin up to look into my eyes. She would give me a slight smile of approval but never an embrace. She seemed to give her dogs more affection than she did to me.

Oh, how I miss my Hebrew family!

*****

One day, in my loneliness, I asked my Egyptian mother, "May I go back and visit the Hebrew family that raised me during my first twelve years?"

I was always careful to never say I *knew* who my true mother was as that might put her and my family in danger. I longed for mother, father, Aaron, and Miriam. I longed for warm arms around me. I longed for a friendly face. I longed for the simple food cooking over the open fireplace. I longed for *love*.

Hatshepsut looked at me with narrowing eyes and gave me a reply that was cold and forceful. She didn't yell at me but spoke with a clinched jaw and with the impact of a very powerful woman that sent chills down my back.

"No! Moses, you belong *here* now! You are *my* son, the Prince of Egypt, who will become Pharaoh and the pride of our nation." Then in a more tender voice, she asked me, "Moses, have you been mistreated? Have you been neglected? Haven't you been given *all the privileges* of a royal inheritance?"

"Yes, Mother… Your Highness," I said with a bow. "Through your influence, I have received more privileges and respect than I ever expected in my life. It is just…well… I would just like for that kind Hebrew woman to see how much I have grown, how much I have learned, and how my voice has recently changed. That I am becoming a *man*."

"Moses, I understand your desire, but remember your rightful place in this dynasty. You will one day sit on the throne as a powerful Pharaoh, the son of Ra, and the king of Egypt."

Then changing her tone and mood again, she snappishly added, "Forget about those people! They can't help you now! Don't ever request that again!"

I never did!

Chapter 5

Royal Education

As years passed, my days were busy and filled with learning and training. I learned well the Egyptian language—spoken and written. I studied history, politics, maps, and Egyptian power. My training included fighting with swords, spears, bows, and knives. I was given the highest level of military and civil instruction, and I became very powerful and skilled in contact fighting. To all practical appearances, I was *totally* Egyptian. My head was shaved, and I wore the clothes and jewelry appropriate for my station and status.

My favorite training, though, was horsemanship. When I was given a beautiful thoroughbred stallion, I was told his name was Emir, which means prince and ruler. His color was a shimmering light bay with a long flowing black tail that almost reached the ground, and he had a silky black mane. His nose was a velvety black, and the lower portions of his strong legs were black. He was so beautiful!

I felt *free* to whisper into Emir's ears my most private thoughts and fears. He couldn't understand my words, of course, but he always bobbed his head and gave me a comforting nicker. Being royalty and the Prince of Egypt, I was always treated with respect, and sometimes fear, but I never felt any *love*. Emir, however, didn't know me as anything but a man. Just a man, not a prince, but I felt *love* from him. There was absolutely nothing I needed physically, yet I longed for true human affection.

Again, I felt *free* while riding this magnificent and swift stallion through the countryside. I felt conflicted being part of this powerful kingdom, albeit through adoption. Yet during my travels, I was not exactly *free*. I was always accompanied by soldiers and guards for my "protection." Eventually, I became a general in Pharaoh's Army and was greatly respected for my strength and ability. This also provided more freedom to ride Emir alone.

I did all that was expected of a Prince of Egypt and the next Pharaoh, except bow down to their numerous gods and idols. There were so many gods, even the priests didn't know their numbers, but they made lavish displays of worshipping the ones they said were the most powerful. The priests tried constantly to make me acquiesce to them and their rituals of idol worship.

They covertly threatened me, saying, "Moses, if you reject the mysteries of our national religion, you could be disowned by your mother, Hatshepsut, and Thutmose I, our Pharaoh! You could lose your position as Prince of Egypt and the next *king* of Egypt."

However, only because of my current royal status was my resistance *somewhat and reluctantly tolerated*.

Hatshepsut was the first born of Thutmose I and rightful heir to the throne that I would inherit through her. When her father died, Hatshepsut's campaign to have me sit *with* her on the throne of Egypt failed. The lesser son of Thutmose I (named Thutmose II), by a secondary wife, was a very young child but was made coregent with Hatshepsut. To secure his right to rule as Pharaoh of Egypt, Thutmose II eventually married Hatshepsut, his half-sister. It was obvious, however, that Hatshepsut was the real controlling power in Egypt. In fact, during official duties, she wore the clothes and headdress of the ruling Pharaohs, even to the wearing of a false beard.

With constant responsibilities and close contact with those teaching or serving me, I was extremely limited to any *free* time to myself. Sometimes, however, while riding my beautiful Emir, I would secretly visit my Hebrew family in the slave quarters.

On one occasion, my entourage and I traveled several days to lower Egypt where I saw the spectacular and majestic pyramids. I was astonished that men could build such structures. *Were they built by slave labor?*

After another day of travel, we were at the point where the Nile split into many smaller rivers making this land rich and fertile. This was Goshen, the land given to Israel and his sons. It was now a slave camp. Up and down the Nile, from Goshen to Thebes, I saw the living conditions and cruel bondage of my people. It seemed that these Hebrews could not last much longer if something wasn't done for them.

As a young boy, I was protected by the Egyptian guards against any brutality toward me or my Hebrew mother. However, I remember that my father occasionally came home with bleeding lashes on his back that my mother treated with her homemade ointment for healing. I often saw streaks on the cheeks of my brother and sister where tears had washed away the dirt and grime from their faces. I felt guilty, but secretly glad, that I was given special protection from this. I could not help but see the pain and suffering my family and those around me felt.

From my earliest childhood, I was often told, "Yahweh has a purpose for saving your life as a baby in the basket floating on the river. *You* will lead our people out of Egypt and back to Canaan."

A plan began to form in my mind.

The Israelites far outnumber the Egyptians. If I can somehow rally them and train them to fight, we could defeat the Egyptian Army. But they are slaves without weapons or training and weakened by strenuous labor and poor nutrition. Or is it my destiny to be the king of Egypt and let my people return to the promised land of Canaan? I need wisdom, and I will plead with God to help me know what to do.

Hatshepsut seemed to notice a change evolving in me, a distance, a remoteness, and a melancholy mood.

"Moses, what is going on? You seem withdrawn and indifferent and yet somehow restless. What is happening, Moses? Talk to me! I *demand* to know!"

Yes, Hatshepsut was a powerful woman and Pharaoh and could "demand" anything she wanted. Opposing her could mean punishment—even death.

As much as I respected her and hated to damage our relationship, I realized that my sympathies toward the Israelites would eventually draw a sword between us. *A dangerous and possibly deadly sword.* I tried to reassure her that I was fine.

"I just need to acknowledge my vast responsibilities and dedicate myself to them."

She seemed to understand my statement of "responsibilities" to mean being the next king of Egypt. But my true meaning was my responsibilities toward *my* people—my hurting and enslaved people throughout Egypt.

"I am very proud of you, Moses. You have grown to be a strong and handsome man—the best of Egypt and our future Pharaoh. Someday, you will sit with me on this throne until the day comes that you, alone, will be the king of the most powerful nation of the world."

Since she and the young Thutmose II are co-regents of Egypt, I don't know if she can arrange for me to sit with her on the throne or even become the next Pharaoh. But then, anything is possible in this powerful and dangerous dynasty.

Looking at me with a smile on her scarlet lips, she added, "By the way, how is it going with you and Nefertari? She is beautiful and obviously captivated by you. She is from a strong family with royal lineage and would make a suitable wife for you. Perhaps you should take some time away from your duties and pursue this graceful Egyptian flower. She is a stunning lotus."

Should take some time…? Is this a mild suggestion or a concealed demand?

Smiling, I bowed respectfully at Hatshepsut, the most powerful woman and Pharaoh of all Egypt. How could she know what I meant by my statement of understanding my "responsibilities"? How could she know my heart and my pain for my family, the pull I feel to release the Hebrews from their Egyptian bondage and slavery? I took her beringed right hand in both of mine and gave it a long and tender kiss. A delicate kiss that pleased her, but it was an emotional kiss that tore a hole in my heart. With another respectful bow, I slowly backed out of the throne room.

Walking away, I almost staggered down the marble steps with my mind racing wildly. As the Prince of Egypt, I often had beautiful women, who were heavily painted, perfumed, and jeweled, buzzing around me in the palace. Their attentions were to attract my desire for one, or more, of them. Did they *love* me or *love* my position?

As was *suggested* by Hatshepsut, and for a while, I spent more time with the beautiful and captivating Nefertari. We walked in the beautiful gardens—gardens that were watered and cared for by *Hebrew* slaves. We strolled the stables of the magnificent horses—stables and horses that were cleaned and groomed by *Hebrew* slaves. We cruised the Nile River powered by strength of *Hebrew* galley slaves. Everywhere I looked, the beauty and elegance of Egypt was due to the hard slave labor of my own people, the Hebrews. Yet for a while, the essence of Nefertari distracted and lingered in my mind.

How can I help these Hebrews—truly help them? Are they able and willing to follow my lead in fighting against their cruel taskmasters and mighty nation? They know me only as a powerful general in the king's Army and the future Pharaoh. They don't see me as anything but Egyptian. Therefore, they would naturally distrust and fear me!

Oh, God, if I am to save my people and return them to Canaan as my Hebrew mother often said to me, grant me the wisdom and the courage for such a plan. Please tell me what to do.

Moses, Prince of Egypt

Chapter 6

THE ABDICATION

A short time later, I decided to cast my lot with the Hebrews—my people. I desired to live and work among them. I would abdicate my royal position as Prince of Egypt and future Pharaoh, which also meant that I would have to renounce my adoption by my Egyptian mother. I struggled severely over this decision.

What is the best way to announce my resolution to Hatshepsut, the strongest co-regent and powerful ruler over all Egypt?

Breaking this announcement to her was harder than any conflict I had yet encountered, and all my training did not prepare me for this!

With my wildly beating heart and sweaty palms, I went to Hatshepsut's well-guarded and lavished apartment. The guard outside knocked twice on her door. He waited several moments and knocked again. Slowly, the door was opened a crack by one of her ladies in attendance. Upon seeing me, she looked back into the room.

"The prince is here, Your Highness."

Several minutes later, I was given permission to enter.

This apartment was large and decorated with the finest of Egyptian artfulness. Silks, gauzy curtains, plush pillows, colorful settees, and embellished marble floors scattered occasionally with animal skins or furs. Her sleek dogs were ever alert to any aggressive movement toward their mistress. Their jeweled collars made a stunning contrast to their ebony coats. Their long, narrow muzzles and pointed ears reminded me of Anubis—the god of embalming and the dead. Anubis was the Egyptian god that was sometimes depicted with the body of a man and the head of a dog.

Hatshepsut had several young women dressed in delicate pale blue attending her—like bees to the queen bee. Soft music from a stringed harp drifted in from a distant room. I had rarely been in this impressive room—a beautiful room that shut out all the ugliness of slave labor, starvation, beatings, and death. Yet this gentle-appearing and sweet-spoken woman standing before me had the ability to transform into a tyrant in an instant. From benevolent to malevolent. From sweet to bitter. From loving to hatred in the blink of an eye. Yet I knew she admired the respect I had earned from the people of Egypt, and she wanted the best for me.

I approached this powerful woman with the highest esteem due to any commanding Pharaoh. I attired myself as royalty, as the Prince of Egypt, heir to the throne of the strongest nation of the world. Bowing extremely low, I waited for her to acknowledge my presence.

"Moses! Moses, *my* prince! Look at you! Dressed in your finest and looking every bit the Royal Prince of Egypt. Come closer. Let us talk. You obviously have something important to say. Your wish is my command."

With a barely distinguishable flick of her hand, all of her attendants quickly left the room. In front of her lavish sofa, she continued to stand on her dais, making her still several inches shorter than me.

My speech was often hesitant and awkward, especially under stress. Oh, how I wanted to express myself and my desires with *dignity*—without stuttering.

Bowing low again, I said, "Your Highness, Mother. It is an honor to be in your presence. This is truly a magnificent apartment made exquisite only by a graceful and elegant jewel."

"Moses, Moses, my prince. Your words flatter me."

Stepping down from her dais, she extended her hand toward me as her dogs became tense and watched my every move.

"Oh great Pharaoh, live forever. I have made…"

"Moses, stop! I am not sitting on the throne now! Stop with the formalities. Just tell me, your mother, what is on your mind."

"Yes, yes, you are right." Bowing again, I added, "I have made an extremely hard decision. I am conflicted and at war within myself. I know I have been given the rights and privileges above all other men in Egypt…next to the Pharaohs. I also know that my blood is not Egyptian. It is Hebrew!"

There it was—that ugly word in the eyes and hearts of all Egyptians, *Hebrew.* They were a hated people, good only for slavery, for the *purpose and benefit* of Egypt. They were a people who were despised and easily extinguished if they became useless or unable to toil under the lash. Yet their skills had helped to make Egypt beautiful and strong.

"Please forgive me, but I have seen the bondage of *my* people and feel deeply for them. I can no longer pretend that had I not been rescued from the river by you, I would have been killed by the decree of the king or condemned as a slave of Egypt and treated as cruelly as they were then… and now."

Hatshepsut's face was as expressionless as one of the stone gods she worshipped, which held a prominent place in her apartment. Taking a deep breath and gaining more confidence, I continued.

"I can never thank you enough for all you have done for me. Out of my deepest respect for you, I am *regretfully* renouncing my position as Prince of Egypt and casting my lot with the Hebrews in Goshen."

At first, this powerful Pharaoh of Egypt just looked at me with confusion in her gray-green eyes.

"Renouncing? Renouncing? What are you talking about, Moses? You *cannot* do that! You are *not* Hebrew. You are *Egyptian,* and you are *my son*! *My son!*"

Standing straight and stately, Hatshepsut stared directly into my eyes, revealing that there was no greater power in the world but hers. Not surprisingly, this formidable woman became furious with this unexpected announcement. Her confusion gave way to anger. It seemed that her exquisite facial makeup began to crack with intense crevices—crevices that seemed to become deep, threatening volcanic eruptions. I had seen her intensely angry before, but this was beyond belief—beyond any control! She began to shriek with outrage and terror, which caused the guards to come running into her apartment.

She screamed at them, "Get out! Get out!" Then turning her furry onto me, she yelled, "That is impossible! That is crazy! You must be insane! Moses, you *cannot* leave your responsibility as heir to the throne of Egypt. I won't allow it! Do you hear me? Believe me, and hear me *well*, Moses! I would rather have you *killed* than see you abandon your duties and obligations and just walk away as if all your endowments have meant *nothing* to you. You are no longer Hebrew—*you are Egyptian! Egyptian!*

A pain ran through my body as if I had been bitten by Uraeus, the cobra god ordaining the headdress this Pharaoh wore while sitting on her throne. I wanted to keep my eyes locked to hers, but I couldn't. I looked toward the floor as all slaves did when confronted by their overseers. I didn't have the verbal or emotional mastery to withstand her forceful and fearful tirade.

After a few moments of deadlock silence, I hoped this fierce Pharaoh did not see me flinch as she reached out to touch my cheek as she used to do when I was a child.

In a surprisingly compassionate voice, she said, "Moses, Moses. What do you know about working in the mud pits or making bricks? What will become of you in the slave camps? You have *never* had a lash to your back. You have *never* known hardship or deprivation. Do you want that? Do you *really* want that? What *good* would come of it? Do you think sharing the Hebrews' plight will relieve their troubles?"

What could I say? She was right, of course. I had never been flogged or severely punished. Yes, I had been *cautiously reprimanded* for my refusing to bow to the many Egyptian gods, but I knew nothing of harsh discipline. Was she weakening my resolve to join the Hebrews? *No! No!*

I remembered the words of my Hebrew mother. "Yahweh saved you, Moses, to deliver us from the Egyptians and return us to Canaan, the land of our fathers."

No! I cannot weaken and deny my people.

After Hatshepsut's brief and tender warning for my future if I were to step into the mud pits, the fury in her eyes returned. First her eyes and then her whole body.

"What will become of *me*?" she screamed. "Have I meant *nothing* to you? What have those *pathetic and filthy* slaves ever done for you? Nothing! Did they make you a great army general, a powerful commander…second only to the monarch of the richest and strongest nation in the world? No, Moses! I won't allow it! Do you hear me? I simply will *not* allow it!" After a few moments, in a low and threatening voice, she added, "I would rather see you *dead* than have you abandon your responsibilities as Prince of Egypt and the next Pharaoh."

Then, picking up an exquisite blue and gold vase, she threw it across the room, making it shatter on the marble floor. The broken shards stopped at the feet of one of the stone gods. Her dogs stood at attention with their muscles taut, waiting the *command*. She was red faced and trembling with hate in her eyes. The volcano had erupted and threatened to destroy me.

I could see how much this wounded and devastated Hatshepsut, my *adopted* mother. I ached to pull her into my arms and give her a mother/son embrace. I yearned to thank her sincerely for all she had done for me. It was this princess that pulled me out of the crocodile-infested river. Through her, I was given all luxuries and a royal inheritance.

As I stepped toward this beautiful royal queen, the co-Pharaoh of all Egypt, I saw a dagger clenched tightly in her hand. Knuckles white with strength and anger! Thinking better of getting too close, I bowed respectfully to her. With a heavy heart, I slowly backed away to leave the room as she again screamed my name.

"Moses, *Moses!*"

Before exiting, a heavy object whizzed past my bowed head and broke into pieces as it hit the door behind me. I realized that my future life, for good or bad, had her influence on me.

FROM HAUGHTY TO HUMBLE

Hatshepsut

Chapter 7

The Mud Pits/The Murder

It was tremendously painful to see Hatshepsut so hurt and violently angry at me. But I felt a *calling*, a God-given mission. I would rather be the *savior* of my people than the king of Egypt. I would *release* the Israelites from their bondage and return them to Canaan as was promised to them many years ago. I wasn't exactly sure *how* I could accomplish this daunting task, but I was a mighty general and knew the tactics of war. Of course, I also realized, sadly, that many of the Israelites would undoubtedly die in a battle against the Egyptian Army—but then, there are always casualties in *any* war.

After arriving at the slave camp in my royal robes and on my regal stallion, I saw again the wretched living conditions of my people. It tore at my heart to see their poverty especially beside the riches and luxury to which I was accustomed. Still looking like a royal prince, I went directly to my family's small home with the straw-covered dirt floor. I told Mother, Aaron, and Miriam of my plans to join their lives of bondage.

"I have abdicated my position as Prince of Egypt and future Pharaoh. I am putting together a plan to release you, and all my people, from this despicable servitude to Egypt. I will need your help to assemble the elders to meet with me."

The sky was blue, the breeze felt comfortable in the warm sun. I was confident that I could fulfill Yahweh's plan (whatever it was) for His children to leave Egypt and return to the "promised land." In my excitement and enthusiasm, I expected my brother and sister to rally behind me joyously at the thought of *freedom*. But Aaron just crossed his arms and looked at me with suspicion and doubt. Miriam turned her head and walked to the pot of stew hanging from a hook over the fireplace.

Silence! I searched for their support and encouragement, but I found only skepticism and disbelief. *How can they distrust me? I am their brother after all. Their brother and their blood! Don't they realize what I can do for them? Don't they realize what I have given up for them?*

Finally, breaking the cold silence, Aaron said with sarcasm in his tone, "Impossible! Do you expect everyone to unite behind you and just *walk* out of Egypt? What is your proposal? Is it realistic? Is it even *reasonable*? Can you explain this plan of yours to me…a simple man and a broken slave of Egypt? What is it, Moses? If you have abdicated the throne as you said, what power do you currently possess? What authority? Yes, we see you standing there in your fancy royal clothes, but do you *really* think you are like us *now*?"

Aaron's verbal attack shook me to the core. I felt like a date palm tree without the fruit, tall and stately but worthless. Again, I felt like his baby brother trying to impress him. I was at a loss for words as I stood before him adorned in my rich finery, but naked and ashamed. Stripped of royalty and stripped of kinship!

Truthfully, I did *not* have a valid plan of action in mind. This was, after all, a recently devised and developing objective. All the same, I *tried* to reassure them, but my family's skepticism filled the room with dark and foreboding shadows, making it difficult to breathe. No wind, not even a breeze, for my sails.

Don't they understand that I have given up power and prestige to join them...and help them? If I can't convince my own family, how can I rally all Israel? Is Aaron right? Am I wrong? If this is a horrendous mistake on my part, should I return to Egypt and ask Hatshepsut for forgiveness? Is it too late to return?

Finally, my mother gave me the first, and only, encouraging words.

"I knew it, Moses! I *knew* it! Yahweh will use you to save us and take us back to Canaan as He promised!" Throwing her arms around me, she said, "I knew it! Praise be to our God!"

If I imagined that the Israelites might not trust or follow me as the Prince of Egypt and a powerful general in the Army, I also soon discovered they would not listen to me working beside them in the slave mud pits. I was no better off than they were. My work now as a Hebrew slave was hard and hot. Water and nutrition were inadequate for our hard labor.

What have I done to myself? What have I done to help my people? Nothing! I gave up everything for nothing! Hatshepsut was right!

I now felt the terrible sting of a lash to my strong and unscarred back. The soldiers and overseers under my *previous* charge did not treat me any better than the rest of the sweating slaves. And perhaps under the command of Hatshepsut, I was occasionally treated worse. This continued for a season until I had almost given up hope and often wondered if I had made a terrible mistake. I prayed for wisdom the way I was taught as a child by my mother. I prayed for the opportunity to see a way of freedom for my family and *all* Israel.

*****

On my way home from the mud pits at the end of an exhausting day, I saw a strong Egyptian foreman savagely kicking and flogging an old man.

Jumping into action, I grabbed the Egyptian's arm and asked, "Why are you beating this old man? What has he done to deserve such treatment?"

"How dare you take a hold of my arm you Hebrew scum! I will do the same to you. Besides, I don't need a reason to beat a dog! He is just an old dog...a worthless *Hebrew dog*!"

Something inside of me snapped. Rage and hate! I grabbed the foreman by the throat, and with a couple of quick jabs of his own dagger, he was dead! I had killed many men in war and had injured many in hand-to-hand combat, but I had never purposely killed anyone with such *hatred*. At first, I felt justified by my actions. Then fear overwhelmed me. I had killed an Egyptian and not long after I had renounced my royal position as Prince of Egypt!

The old Hebrew cried, "No...no! Look what you did! You killed him! You killed an Egyptian! What is going to happen to us now?"

At that, the old man ran away and left me standing alone with the dead and bloodied body at my feet. I was sure no one had seen what I had done, so I quickly dug a hole in the sand and buried the offender of my kinsman.

One Egyptian down—but only one!

*****

The very next day, I came across a couple of Hebrew men fighting. Wanting them to settle their dispute, I stepped in and accused the malefactor of wrongdoing and insisted they resolve their quarrel.

Then the aggressor raised his voice and asked, "Who made you judge over us? What gives you the right to interfere? Are you going to kill me too as you killed the Egyptian last night?"

As I looked around, I realized that several men had witnessed this accusation toward me. My secret was no longer hidden in the sand. My crime was uncovered and obvious for everyone to see. It felt like his blood was still on my hands and seeping up through the sand. There was no hole deep enough to hide my guilt and my crime. Instead of rallying behind me to overthrow the Egyptians, my kinsmen now accused me—and feared me. Couldn't they see I was doing this *for them*? All too soon, I was sure that Hatshepsut and Thutmose II would hear about this too.

Yes, Pharaoh Thutmose II was informed about the killing, and I heard that he was furious! Because of my previous popularity in the palace and among the soldiers, he now became afraid I would try to overthrow him and take over the throne and rule Egypt. I don't know if Hatshepsut added to his fears or not, but her threat that she would rather see me "killed" than see me leave my royal responsibilities may have even ignited his edict to have me put to death. When I became aware of this order, I knew I needed to leave Egypt as soon as possible—now!

It was obvious to me that I was *not* the one destined by God to lead the Israelites out of Egypt and back to Canaan. I was a colossal failure and now a fugitive. In my pride, I had made boastful and obviously impossible plans for my family and all of Israel. It broke my heart to see the disappointment in my mother's eyes.

Knowing my life was in danger, I kissed my mother goodbye and gathered up some personal items I might be able to use or exchange for needed provisions. I also gathered as much food and water as my family could spare. I headed north, out of Thebes, then east—keeping the sun generally ahead of me in the morning and at my back in the evening. I didn't know where I was going, but I needed to get out of Egypt and into the possible safety of Arabia.

CHAPTER 8

FUGITIVE TO MIDIAN

I ran or walked as fast as I could for many days with very little rest, always looking over my shoulder for signs of anyone following me. The days were sweltering hot, but the nights were often cold. Carrying my heavy warm cape during the heat of the day was exhausting, yet I found it barely sufficient to keep me warm at night. Finally, with near exhaustion, I hid in a cool rocky cave for a day. I dozed fitfully but was afraid of genuine sleep or to build a fire for warmth—always listening for sounds of men or horses.

During all this time, I wondered, "Where did I fail? Why did I fail?" *Obviously, I am not the one destined by God to liberate the Israelites from slavery and bondage as my mother often told me. I am a fugitive from Egypt with a price on my head. God will need to call a more worthy person to take on this daunting responsibility.*

While rationing my food and water, I walked for weeks heading mostly east yet not knowing where I was or where I was going. I saw only desert lizards, scorpions, and vultures flying overhead.

Are they waiting and watching for me to stop...or drop? I had blended into this dry and barren scenery and felt I would soon be part of this lifeless desert. God, is this truly the end of my life? Am I to die in this no-man's land? Alone and anonymous?

I had come so far—far from royal and regal surroundings and far from prestige and prominence. I tried desperately to hold on to God—the God of our fathers, the God I learned about at my mother's knee, and the God I tried to worship and defend in the palace of Pharaoh.

Oh, God...have mercy on me!

My mind began to blur. I had depression and hallucinations. I was losing time, losing direction, and losing purpose. Occasionally, I saw things that I knew were not there. I heard phantom voices condemning me for my pride in thinking I was the "savior" of Israel or condemning me for my murderous act that put a price on my head. I seemed to be going insane. I was exhausted from running and exhausted from guilt, fear, hunger, and thirst. All of my provisions were gone.

I am going to die here in this desert.

Suddenly, I realized that my latest "mirage and spirit voices" were curiously real. *Real?* Had I actually come upon a small settlement and village—here in the middle of nowhere? This was no hallucination. Water was my first necessity to relieve my dehydration and soothe my dry throat and cracked lips. At a well, some women were drawing water for their sheep, and seeing my desperate need, they offered me the lifesaving drink. I couldn't remember when water tasted so good—cool, restoring, reviving. My mind began to clear and I could think beyond my desperation.

After drinking my fill and pouring water all over my face and head, I began to feel alive again when some loud and vulgar shepherds arrived and threatened to drive the women and their sheep from the well. Still feeling weak and tired and leaning against the stones around the well, I mustered a commanding voice and demanded these ruffians to leave until the women were finished at the well. Laughing at me, it was obvious they were not impressed until I stood tall and drew my Egyptian sword—one of the few things I still possessed from my past life. Seeing that I was serious and taking on a threatening stance, they backed away and left the women to finish caring for their sheep.

I felt refreshed by the cool water, but I was still exhausted and famished, so I sat back down beside the well. Timidly, the women introduced themselves as sisters, the daughters of one man named Jethro, the priest of Midian. One of the sisters cautiously approached and gave me some bread and dried mutton to eat. Mostly, they just stood and watched me until I put my head back against the well and pretended to be asleep. When they left, I heard quiet giggling and whispers of returning later to finish watering their sheep. Eventually, feeling slightly stronger and so grateful for their kindness, I offered to help these women draw water for their sheep.

After the sheep were safely put in their shelter for the rest of the late afternoon, the women went home and told their father what had happened.

"Father, a man, an *Egyptian*, drove away some crude and abusive shepherds from the well. After we gave him some water and a little food, he helped us water our sheep."

"*Egyptian?* Are you sure he is Egyptian? Hmm…if that is true, he's a long way from his country!"

"We think so, Father. He is tall and looks very strong with authority. He wears gold bands on his arms, and his shoes are laced up to his knees. Also, he has a very threatening and impressive-looking sword."

"Well, if he was kind to you, my daughters, we should ask him to stay and eat with us this evening."

Being weak with hunger and many days of desert travel, I gladly accepted the invitation for a good meal. Food! Yes! Walking into the tent of my host, I was impressed with its elegance and dimensions. There were many plush pillows and richly patterned carpets. It was reminiscent of Hatshepsut's elegant apartment but without the cold marble floors and stone gods. The hanging oil lamps gave an invitingly warm glow to the surroundings. My host introduced himself as Jethro, the priest of Midian, and encouraged me to make myself comfortable.

"Please, sit, relax, and rest while we wait for our meal."

Still standing, I looked around at this richness—and my dirty clothes. I felt unworthy to make myself "comfortable" on such finery. My host clapped his hands, and two servants hurried into the room with two basins of water and towels.

Am I expected to wash myself in front of everyone in this room?

Again, my host said, "Please," and indicated with his hands for me to sit. One of the basins was for me to wash my hands and face, while the other was used by a servant to wash my dirty and cracked feet. A soothing oil was then applied, and soft slippers were given to me—which were really too small. My host clapped his hands again, and another servant approached and stood in front of me with a clean cloak for me to wear. Not since I had left the courts of Egypt had I been treated with such kindness. But this thoughtfulness seemed genuine, not because of my past royal status. Certainly, he knew nothing of me—or my history.

A great abundance of food was brought on large silver trays. It was such enjoyable cuisine, the best I had eaten in a *very long time*. Due to my extreme hunger, my dinner manners were a bit uncultured and boorish—certainly not fit for royalty or an example of my strict upbringing. Watching me devour my meal like some ravaged animal, the daughters of Jethro began to giggle. All eyes were on me! Feeling embarrassed and with my mouth full of meat, I looked around and mumbled an apology for my ill-mannered behavior, which brought on more laughter. I joined in the laughter. It was comfortable and welcoming here, and I was invited to stay the night.

Jethro, the priest of Midian, said he was a worshipper of the true God, Jehovah. He spoke Hebrew but with a strange dialect. Since the last thirty years of my life I spoke primarily Egyptian, my Hebrew was also peculiar and a little difficult for him to understand. However, if we spoke slowly to each other, we were able to communicate well enough.

Jethro was a small man with a long, graying beard and wore a brimless cloth cap on his head. It was hard to ascertain his age, but I thought he might be my senior by about twenty-five years or more. I, on the other hand, was almost a cubit taller than Jethro. I now had a scruffy beard of many weeks old, and the hair on my previously shaved head was growing to show the loose brown curls of my childhood.

After our dinner in Jethro's tent and after his daughters were gone, he began to question me about my past, which I was reluctant to divulge.

Finally, he commented, "Moses… Moses… Hmm. That is an Egyptian name, but you say you are Hebrew? How does that happen?"

How can I explain to him that I am Egyptian and *Hebrew? That doesn't make sense! The two races are incompatible…except for perhaps Joseph, who was the eleventh son of Jacob* and *the vizier for Sesostris III, one of the Pharaohs during the twelfth Egyptian dynasty.*

Seeing my jaw clinched and eyes diverted from him, Jethro didn't press the questioning any further.

His hands slapped down on his legs and said, "Enough for now. You have had a long journey, and you need some rest. With your stomach full, you should sleep well."

Clapping his hands twice, he summoned a servant quickly into our presence.

"Give our guest a comfortable bed for the night, and do not waken him in the morning. We will let him sleep until tomorrow's evening meal."

I stayed a few days in the gracious hospitality of Jethro, the priest of Midian. My guest quarters consisted of a tent comfortably furnished with an Arabian aura of ornate tapestries, cushions, and rich carpets. It was all very impressive and welcoming for a restful night's sleep.

I wished to repay Jethro for his kindness, but what could I give? I had *nothing*—nothing to offer but the strength of my back, a back that now had evidences of the "lash," long and healing stripes of Egyptian rule and power.

*****

My past status as the Prince of Egypt and future Pharaoh afforded me a superior standing. I neither *thanked* nor *asked* for anything—I commanded! I bowed to *no one* except to a Pharaoh. As a powerful general in the Egyptian Army, I could fight, command legions, ride horses, and drive chariots. I was proud of my accomplishments and my power. I even imagined through *my own* strength and ability, *I* could free the Israelites—my people. But now, everything was gone! Everything! It was a *humbling* experience—a new and humiliating understanding for me. My head, which once wore evidence of a high-ranking Egyptian, now wore a price tag and soft brown curls with slight graying at the temples.

Midian was an inviting community in Arabia, nestled between rugged mountains. It was an oasis with plenty of trees, giving shade during hot, sunny days. The nights brought a cool breeze and chirping crickets. The stars seemed brighter because they were not hidden behind the smoke from thousands of Egyptian chimneys. There was enough rain to keep the streams flowing and to provide ample grazing for the sheep and herds. It was a fertile spot in the desert—a beautiful retreat and refuge!

With my growing respect toward Jethro, I always entered his tent with a bow.

"Moses, come in. You are most welcomed here. I trust your stay has been both comfortable and restorative?"

"Yes, Sire, most comfortable. Thank you."

"Sit, Moses. I feel you have something you want to tell me."

"No…well…yes."

Was Jethro expecting me to tell him my *story*? I still was not ready to reveal my past or tell him why I had left Egypt.

"Sire, if you will kindly allow me to stay here in Midian for a while longer and continue to sleep in one of your tents, I will care for your sheep, relieving your daughters to do other and finer obligations."

After saying this, I realized I knew nothing about caring for sheep—Egyptians *despised* shepherds!

I could lead vast Egyptian Armies, but what do I know about these stupid and smelly sheep? But then, what is there to know? All my ancestors are shepherds, so it must be in my blood.

With a returned slight bow from Jethro, I was graciously allowed permission to stay longer in turn for caring for his sheep. I smiled as I heard snickering from the daughters of Jethro outside his tent flap. Apparently, they were pleased too that I would be staying a while longer. Granting my request could not have been because he *needed* help with his sheep. He had many daughters and servants. Perhaps it was out of curiosity of my Egyptian/Hebrew past. At any reason, I now had a welcoming place to stay for a while longer.

At first, the sheep scattered at my presence and my voice.

FROM HAUGHTY TO HUMBLE

I was advised, "You must talk *gently* to them. They will eventually know your voice and learn to trust and follow you."

This learning experience was almost funny—vastly different from my training. As a general in the Egyptian Army, I could *shout* my orders, and they would be obeyed. As a shepherd, I would have to speak softly, lead and protect them.

This will try my patience—the patience I am sorely lacking!

Moses, Fugitive in Midion

CHAPTER 9

HISTORY REVEALED/ PROPOSAL TO ZIPPORAH

During my stay in Midian, I became attracted to one of Jethro's daughters by the name of Zipporah. She had very dark skin, black hair, hazel eyes, and stunningly beautiful. I was mystified by her. She was nothing like the heavily adorned, perfumed, and scantily dressed Nefertari or the other Egyptian women who constantly surrounded me in the palace. Zipporah was strong when she cared for the sheep yet tender with the young lambs. She could speak with confidence yet express tenderness in the most captivating way. She was the leader of her sisters yet humble with her authority. I began to love her very much, and although she never indicated any *open* feelings toward me, I *felt* her quiet affection, which was not like the aggressive and flirtatious attentions I received in the palace from Egyptian maidens.

When time allowed, we spent private and discreet times talking and getting to know each other better. While tending the sheep, she would often bring me some refreshments of fruit, meat, and cool water. Then we would seek out some shade to talk and laugh together. Her voice and laughter sounded genuine, not the forced or faked laugh of the painted women I was used to seeing. This was a new and interesting experience for me.

After several months, my love for Zipporah grew stronger, and I wanted to marry her. That would make me deliriously happy. I especially wanted her to be happy—and happy to be my *wife*. But what did I have to offer her or her father? I had nothing! No bride price! The only price I had was the one on my *head*!

If I were to ask Zipporah to marry me, I must first get the permission and blessing from Jethro. The only thing I could offer was my hard work and my promise to love and support his daughter. I felt like what Jacob must have felt, promising to work for Rachel. But the dark cloud hanging over my past as a fugitive from Egypt might close the door!

With fluttering in my heart and heaviness in my feet, I went to Jethro's tent to talk to the father of my beloved. As I stepped inside, I saw that he was heavily engrossed in a collection of accounting ledgers. He was a wealthy and ethical man with many servants, who were thankful for his recognition of their attendance to him and his family. He appreciated their dedicated work and paid them accordingly.

As I considered returning later when he was not so engaged, he looked up, "Moses, come in! Come in!"

"Jethro, Sire, you have been extremely generous to me during my stay here in Midian while caring for your sheep. I have been welcomed into your family as you would a brother or a son. Thank you! While you have granted my stay, I have grown to admire and love your daughter, Zipporah."

"Moses, let us both sit and talk."

After Jethro reclined on a large cushion, I chose a smaller pillow to sit on with my legs crossed in front of me. With the stress building in my body and throat, I sent a quick and silent request to Yahweh that my words would not be stuttering or clumsy.

"Sire, before I ask Zipporah to be my wife, I know I must first ask for your permission. Before you consent to or deny my marriage to your daughter, you undoubtedly need to know everything about me and my past life...who I am and why I am here. I will answer all of your questions and hold back nothing from you."

"Yes, Moses, I have *many* questions. I must admit the way you carry yourself, you convey an aura of being born to privilege. I am very curious of your past. As you have said, you are both Egyptian *and* Hebrew! How can that be?"

"Indeed...so where do I start?"

"The beginning, Moses. Start at the *beginning*!"

"The beginning? As far back as the 'beginning'?" I questioned.

Groaning inside my soul, I knew I must tell him everything: how I was born to Hebrew slave parents in Egypt; how I was adopted by the Princess of Egypt; how I was raised in the courts of the king of Egypt and destined to be the next Pharaoh; how, through my pride, I thought I could save my people, the Hebrews; how I made a foolish act by abdicating the thrown and casting my lot with the slaves of Egypt; how I killed an Egyptian in hate; and how I fled for my life and ended here in Midian.

"Well, it all began over forty years ago when I was born to a slave family near Thebes of Egypt."

Jethro and I talked all night and into the dawning of the next day. Both of us were exhausted.

Finally, Jethro said, "We need some rest, Moses. Both of us! And I need to consider all that I have learned. Tonight, after our evening meal, we will talk again."

He stood, put his hand on my shoulder, and walked out into the cool morning air by the well. During the long night, Jethro had not given me any impression of his approval or disapproval.

Had I been denied the honor of marrying his daughter? Had he sealed my fate of wandering in some wilderness...alone? I guess I will know tonight.

After talking to Jethro the whole night long and holding back nothing of my life, I felt stripped naked. I had nothing left to give, nothing left to share, except my desire to marry his daughter, an event I dreamed about but for which I felt totally unworthy. I had no desire for any food for fear it might not stay down. My day was stressful for lack of sleep, lack of food, and for awaiting Jethro's decision after the evening meal. I avoided Zipporah that day for many confusing reasons.

Am I worthy? If I am denied the honor of proposing to my beloved, what will I do? I can't stay here in Midian. Where will I go? Go alone! I fully understand "alone." Growing up surrounded by many attentive servants, soldiers, and women, there was no real companionship. No love! Yes, I understand "alone"!

When our evening meal was brought to us on large silver platters laden with meat, bread, and fresh fruit, I wasn't hungry even though I hadn't eaten all day. My stomach was tied in knots, and I felt light-headed. There was polite talk and glances around the room as if everyone knew what was coming next. Finally, after our evening meal, which seemed to take forever, Jethro stood up and motioned for me to stand too. Standing before this man with the power to approve or reject my petition was reminiscent of my standing in front of Hatshepsut, Pharaoh of Egypt. Both held my future in their hands.

"Moses, you came to us from the West, weak and hungry, and obviously with a previous life full of questions and mystery. A life you were reluctant to divulge, but I saw in you a man of strength and integrity. Forgive me if I am speaking out of turn, but you have requested my permission to ask for Zipporah's hand in marriage. Correct?"

My mouth was dry, and I had to clear my throat to answer a feeble and stuttering.

"Y…yes."

I quickly glanced at the beautiful woman whom I wanted for my wife, wishing my "yes" was louder, stronger, and more convincing! She put her hand to her lips, but I could tell by her eyes that she was smiling, but she quickly looked away.

"Moses, last night, you revealed to me your story, your troubled past, your reasons for being here, and your desire to marry my daughter, Zipporah.

"You come with nothing but a troublesome history that is potentially dangerous for my daughter. Your most recent history reveals that you were living among cruel Egyptians and idol worshippers. Your worship of the Hebrew God, Yahweh, is probably, and understandably, fragile. But I see in you a delicate faith of the God of our fathers, which, in time, can grow stronger. Moses, you must *first* tell my daughter everything you have told me about yourself. Then, *if* she accepts your proposal, I will give my approval and my blessing."

Snickering suddenly broke out from the women in this elaborately decorated tent dining room. My knees almost buckled under me, and my heart nearly flew out of my chest. I was both elated and terrified. I wanted to sing and shout to the world, but my tongue stuck to the roof of my mouth.

Looking at Zipporah, I nodded and whispered, "We will talk tomorrow."

That night after dinner, I went to my tent. As sleepy and exhausted as I was, sleep evaded me for many hours. I tossed and turned. I wondered if my history, and the possible danger it imposed on me and any family I might have, would cause Zipporah to deny my request for marriage. Jethro knew my story, my history—my *whole* history. Should I *soften* it a bit for her sake?

No! I will be completely honest with Zipporah. I will not try to control the outcome as I have done so often in the past. I will pull down the mask. I will be totally honest and vulnerable.

The next day, the whole story of my life was repeated in detail to Zipporah. It was exhausting having to tell my life's history again, but with her tender look, and the occasional tears in the eyes of my beloved, I was encouraged to continue.

"Zipporah, my beloved, I know I have nothing to give to you but my love and devotion. I will do my best to protect you from any harm. I will work hard to support and build a home for you… for us. I am asking from the bottom of my most sincere heart, will you marry me?"

"Yes…*yes*!"

After accepting my proposal of marriage, and blessings from Jethro, Zipporah and I were eventually wed in the elaborate Arabian flair. There were many gifts, elegant and rich foods, music and dancing—all fit for a prince and his princess. My bride was beautiful, and I couldn't keep my eyes off her. We set up our own home near the landholdings of Jethro's compound and eventually had two beautiful sons named Gersham and Eliezer. Life couldn't be better!

Being a father was more enjoyable and more work than I expected. The only real family I knew was my very early life with my mother, Jochebed. Since my father was forced to work as a slave for the Pharaoh from morning until night, I rarely saw him. Egyptian royals didn't raise their own children. It was always the responsibility of the women in the palace harem. What a drastic change for me. Now, I was a father of two beautiful boys—and I was a shepherd! Who knew?

Although I was taught by Jochebed to worship the true God, Jehovah, I had to learn to approach God with humbleness and reverence and not with pride or with the grandiose display I saw toward the Egyptian gods. I also had to appreciate a simple life with the occasional denial of needs. There was a vast difference from my past existence and experience.

I was from prince to pauper, from soldier to shepherd, from reckless to responsible, from power to patience. *From haughty to humble!*

I learned to appreciate the simple life in the Midian desert oasis with my family—and Jethro's sheep! Being alone, and caring for the sheep in the hills and fields, gave me much private time to pray and communicate with Jehovah. I listened to the Spirit of God—and the sheep listened to me! I wrote poetry, history, and music while playing on Jethro's lyre.

I lived many years in the oasis of Midian—the same number of years I lived in Egypt. My two sons were grown and had families of their own. Our life was occasionally harsh but stable with many blessings. We worked hard, caring for and raising a large herd of sheep. We were shearing, skinning, selling, and birthing lambs. Our wool was sold or woven into cloth by the daughters of Jethro and other women of our community. Some of it was dyed and used for ourselves, but most of it was sold to traveling merchants. Jethro became an even wealthier man, who was generous toward me and my family.

Zipporah

CHAPTER 10

THE BURNING BUSH

One day, while watching the sheep on the hillside, I saw a bush burning farther up the mountainside—only the *one* bush! Nothing else around it was burning. A strange sight. The weather was calm. There was no thunder and no lightning, nothing seemed out of the ordinary. What had caused this bush to burn? I determined to take a closer look at this bizarre phenomenon.

As I got closer, a voice from the flames said, *Moses.*

Looking around briefly, I said fearfully, "Yes, here I am."

Take off your sandals because you are standing on holy ground.

"Who are you? Who is t-talking to me?"

I am Jehovah, the God of your fathers, Abraham, Isaac, and Jacob.

Now, I was afraid! Afraid to look at the flames in the bush that occasionally seemed to leap out toward me. The heat was intense. I quickly removed my sandals and covered my face with my cloak.

While on my knees and my face to the ground, I wondered, *What does God want with me? Is He now going to destroy me for killing that Egyptian in hate or thinking I could save my people from their cruel slavery? Or…or…*

A thousand thoughts flashed through my racing confusion.

The voice coming from the fire continued, *I have seen the suffering of My people in Egypt and have heard their cries and know their sorrows. I want to deliver them from the hands of the Egyptians and give them a land filled with milk and honey. And, Moses, I have chosen you to go to Pharaoh. You will lead my children out of Egypt and worship Me on this mountain.*

Terrified, I asked, "Lord, who am I to do such a thing? What you are telling me to d-do is too hard. It's im-impossible!"

I knew that after many years of slavery in Egypt, the Hebrews were nearly destitute of their knowledge of the God of their fathers.

"If I t-tell them that God has sent me to lead them out of Egypt, they will j-just ridicule m-me saying, 'Yeah? You think God spoke t-to you, Moses? Which God? What is His n-name?'"

When the Voice spoke again, the ground shook like a mighty earthquake with huge rocks rolling down the mountain scattering the sheep.

I AM THAT I AM. You will say that "I AM" has sent you!

With my mind spinning and thinking of the difficulties, I said, "Lord, it has been a long t-time! I am not the same m-man that ran from Egypt's king years ago. Or perhaps… I am still the same m-man because I am still afraid. After I killed the Egyptian, even the Hebrews turned against m-me. I was only trying to h-help and start their d-deliverance. But I failed. F-failed miserably! If I return, they will resist me and d-deny that You have spoken or appeared to me! And…and…and what if they want p-proof that you have sent me?"

What is that in your hand, Moses? Your staff? Throw it to the ground!

Still on my knees, I tossed my staff off to the side a few feet away from me. Instantly, it turned into a venomous viper that was rearing its ugly and poisonous head at me. I jumped up and *ran*! Cobras are a symbol of Egypt's deadly power. And now many years after running from Pharaoh, that power continued to threaten me.

Now, pick it up by the tail, was the Voice's command.

After some maneuvering and trying to distract the snake, I was finally able to grab it by the tail. Instantly, it turned back into my shepherd's staff!

After that, the Lord gave me another *proof*. He then said for me to show both of these amazing events to the Israelites in Egypt.

Then they will believe you, Moses.

My mind was spinning with the thought of such a heavy and seemingly impossible responsibility. Then I came up with another excuse for my reluctance.

"Oh, my Lord, it has b-been forty years since I have spoken the language of the Egyptians, and I am s-slow and a-awkward in my speech, which gets worse when I am under s-stressful situations. How can I speak for You if I sound clumsy and gauche?"

Moses, who made your mouth, who made your eyes? Have not I, your God, made you? I will be with your mouth and tell you what to say! Go! Your brother, Aaron, is now on his way to meet you. Together, you will talk to Pharaoh to let my people go on a three days journey out of Egypt to worship me.

Fear still hovered over me. Even with the *proof* that God was able to do as He said, I trembled at the thought. I was now eighty years old and had changed so much from the time I could stand in front of Pharaoh and talk with strength and confidence.

Now, I am afraid. Am I afraid of my weakness! I am afraid that God cannot overcome my deficiencies or my fears. Do I not have enough faith? Should I remind God that both Pharaohs, Hatshepsut and Thutmose II, have ordered my death?

Before leaving the burning bush, many more awesome and fearful instructions were given to me. I was told that Pharaoh would *not* release the children of Israel until numerous and terrible things happened in Egypt.

Finally, God added, *By the way, Moses, those Egyptians who sought to kill you are now dead, and there is a different Pharaoh on the throne. Remember, Moses, I will be with you. Now, go! And you will see now what I will do to Egypt and their worthless gods.*

*****

After telling my father-in-law, Jethro, all that God had spoken to me, he rose to his feet. I also stood. Not being quite tall enough to reach the top of my head for the traditional blessing, he put both of his hands on my shoulders.

"Moses, I am convinced that God has chosen you to lead the Israelites out of Egypt. You just needed to wait for *His* timing and *His* guidance. You are not the same man you were forty years ago who thought you could do this all on your own. Now, you realize you *need* the Great I AM. Go in peace, my son. God will be with you!"

Zipporah and my two sons wanted to go with me, so we packed our mules for the long trip to Egypt. The hot desert travel and overnight stops were a new and tiresome experience for my wife. There was nothing but bleached bones, rocks, lizards, scorpions, and buzzards. My family had many questions. *I* had many questions. Questions without answers! My mind kept thinking about what was in store for me in Egypt. And how would I find my brother, Aaron, in this vast wasteland?

After numerous days of traveling, I saw someone walking toward us—it was my brother! I hardly recognized him. Aaron was only three years older than me, yet he appeared much older and so thin. His eyes looked tired, and his beard was nearly white. But what a wonderful reunion—embraces, kisses, and introductions!

"Moses, I had the strangest dream and the strongest impression. I was told by God to meet you here in this desert. We thought you were dead! What is happening? Why are you here? Are you returning to Egypt?"

"Come! We have much to talk about."

We found some sparse shade beside a large grouping of rocks. We rested, ate, and began sharing our experiences over the past forty years. Aaron and I talked through the night while my wife slept in a makeshift tent and my sons under a lean-to. I told Aaron all that God had instructed *both* of us to do. A daunting and dangerous mission! Aaron related to me all the severely barbaric treatments the Israelites were suffering under Thutmose III, the proud and powerful Pharaoh of Egypt.

In the morning, after a modest breakfast, Aaron and I took a brief nap while my sons packed our mules. After hearing about what was currently happening in Egypt, I realized that my tenderhearted wife would be unable to witness such inhumane treatment. It didn't take much to convince Zipporah that she and our sons should return to Midian especially when she learned that we were not even halfway to Goshen of Egypt. Remembering the words of the I AM that I was to lead His people out of Egypt, I promised to see my family again someday.

Aaron and I continued our travel to Egypt. Our travel was long and tiring, but Aaron and I had much to share and to consider about what the future held. He told me how he had to enlarge the little house I shared with him as a young boy to accommodate his sons, Miriam, and even our father who was *still alive*!

Aaron told me of the Israelites' struggles under this new Pharaoh—the workload, the beatings, the deaths. I felt guilty sharing my blessings of a wonderful wife and sons and living in peace. Guiding and protecting Jethro's sheep, I had learned to be more patient. However, no longer did I wish to take control and liberate the Israelites.

Lord, are You sure I am the right person for such a mission? It is such a daunting responsibility. Lord, give me wisdom and have mercy on me, my brother, and all of your people!

CHAPTER 11

RETURN TO EGYPT

Upon our arrival at Goshen in Egypt, I could see and *feel* the effects of severe slavery. The streets were cluttered with broken pottery, ragged and useless baskets, carcasses of dogs and rats. Suspicion slammed doors or peeked around corners. I was received just as I had predicted—with skepticism and resistance.

The Israelites' worship of Jehovah, the God of their fathers, was weak and tenuous during their over four hundred years in Egypt. Their only resolve was to somehow leave this land, this slavery, and this oppression.

Even the Hebrew elders questioned, "Why are *you*, Moses, after all these years coming back to liberate us? What gives you the authority or the power to defy Pharaoh and our taskmasters? After you defected your right to be king of Egypt, Pharaoh sought to kill you. We thought you were *dead*!"

Then they added, "Why *now,* after forty years? Who is this *God* that you say spoke to you? Did He speak to *us* or to any of our elders? No! Did He speak to your brother, Aaron? No! Tell us, how can we believe you? What is God's *name*?"

"The God of our fathers, Jehovah, is called I AM…the *Great I AM*."

The vast number of the Egyptian gods all had *names*. It seemed to these men that the God who spoke to me should also have a "name." The Egyptians believed their stone gods had general purposes for directing, protecting, or destroying their lives or property. Some of their gods were more powerful than others, and these deities often fought among themselves, even killing one another until another god would raise him or her back to life again. Some of these Egyptian gods married other gods, which produced more gods. Pharaoh was the "Son of Ra," the sun god, which naturally made Pharaoh a god.

Moses before Pharaoh

I showed these doubting elders the miracle of my staff turning into a poisonous snake, which caused them to jump back and out of its danger. Cobras were common and dangerous in Egypt and something to be feared. They also knew that the Pharaoh wore its symbol on his headdress, and *he* was certainly someone to be feared—a king with the power to destroy. After taking the snake by the tail and having it return to my staff, they accused me of witchcraft—*Egyptian witchcraft!*

Next, I put my hand and arm inside my cloak. Upon pulling it back out, my arm was white and dead with leprosy. Leprosy was a disease with a death sentence and was believed to be the "judgment of God." They yelled, "He is cursed! *Cursed!* Moses is cursed by God! Stone him!" Quickly, before the first stone was thrown at my head, I returned my arm into the cloak and withdrew it again. A normal and healthy arm appeared and was examined.

At seeing these "signs," a few of the elders finally agreed to go with Arron and me to Pharaoh's court. Accept for the power of God, we were incapable of challenging this powerful king to release his slaves, the Hebrews.

After several days of travel from Goshen to Thebes, this small party of elders accompanied Aaron and me up the wide and impressive steps to Pharaoh's palace. None, except me, had ever been inside this spectacular and intimidating throne room. I understood their uneasiness. I understood their trepidation. I understood their distrust of me. I understood their tenuous faith in the God of our fathers.

As Aaron and I boldly approached Thutmose III, the elders seemed to lag behind with their eyes to the floor, knowing they were not permitted to look directly at Pharaoh, the sun god.

CHAPTER 12

THUTMOSE III

Being Hebrew and living in Midian for forty years, I wore a full beard and longer than shoulder-length hair. Since I was eighty years old, my hair and beard had many streaks of gray, but it was not as white nor was I as balding as my brother, Aaron. Egyptian men were clean-shaven. Only their women had long or tightly braided hair festooned with beads and jewels. I wanted to distinguish myself to Thutmose III with dignity and authority, so I trimmed my beard and shortened my hair. I also attired myself with some of my Egyptian accessories, which I still owned as the former Prince of Egypt.

As Aaron and I, and several Hebrew elders, approached the impressive Egyptian palace, many memories flooded my mind. The stately mansion was *always* impeccably clean because servants swept away the fine powdery dust blown in from the desert winds. The tall and tanned Egyptian guards stood at attention with their shiny shields and spears. Priests in their long, white tunics, with jeweled necks and arms, walked with their heads held high. They always strolled with a reserved aloofness and unapproachable air. There was, of course, a different Pharaoh that I knew forty years ago—the powerful Thutmose III. But very little else had changed in the years since I had left Egypt.

I announced my name to the palace guards and presented our request to speak to the king. A few of the older members of the court remembered me, having been under *my charge* as Commander of the Army and the Prince of Egypt. With a cautious bow, they treated me with utmost respect and expressed their surprise that I was alive. They quietly cautioned me to "be careful." We were not immediately granted audience with the king. Since we were Israelites, and not worthy of any real concern in the royal court, we had to wait over an hour.

Finally, and upon entering the great throne room, I looked around at the grand display of wealth and riches. It all came back to my memory—the gold, the opulence, the gods, the ceremony, and the royal throne that was to be mine, had I not defected. Standing before this proud king, I *endeavored* to convey power and nobility. I did not speak directly to him but looked straight and fearlessly into his piercing jet-black eyes. This, of course, is forbidden by Egyptian law.

Speaking only Hebrew, I told Aaron what to say as God had instructed me to do. Then expressing as eloquently as he could in the Egyptian tongue to Pharaoh, Aaron translated my words,

"We are requesting that you release your slaves, the Israelites living in Goshen and throughout Egypt, to make a three-day journey into the desert to worship and make sacrifices to Jehovah. Our God says, 'Let My people go!'"

First, with an air of amusement and looking around the throne room, he responded, "Ha! You have to be kidding! The Hebrews—*my slaves leave?* Have I gotten this right? You are asking for a three days' journey into the desert, which means three days to return—plus the time spent worshiping your God? No! Ridiculous!"

When the king saw that we didn't back down or cower to him, his face changed to irritation, and he glared directly and intently at me.

"Why are you wanting to take these people from their work? How do you *dare* to ask such a brazen request? I am Pharaoh, Thutmose III, the Son of Ra, and I have built up and increased this kingdom—the largest and strongest in the history of Egypt. My sons and I will surely control and rule the *world*. I have many slaves. All of them, including the Hebrews, *belong to me*! And you want them to leave? No! My answer is *no*! Now, get out! Leave me, and get back to your labors."

Waving his hand, we were instantly dismissed and crudely grabbed by our arms and ushered out at sword point. I wasn't surprised that Pharaoh refused to let the Israelites leave because God told me He would "harden Pharaoh's heart." However, I was not expecting the labor of God's people to be hardened too!

The straw that was used in making the bricks had always been delivered by the foremen. That stopped! The slaves now had to look for and gather the straw for themselves with no decrease in the production of bricks.

Pharaoh told the taskmasters and Hebrew foremen, "These are lazy people! They want to leave and worship their God? This will make this man, Moses, and the others sorry for what they are asking."

With their increased workload and threats from Pharaoh, God's people complained and blamed *me*! Yes, they complained and threatened, saying, "Moses, you have made things worse for us, and our burdens are now harder! You promised that God would deliver us. What has happened to that promise? Moses, leave us! Leave us alone! Go back to…to wherever you have been for the last forty years! Leave us, or Pharaoh will surely kill us!"

Life continued in the hot sun and cloudless sky without even a soft breeze to help cool down their sweltering bodies. The only change was the increased workload, longer days to fulfill the brick quota, and more bleeding stripes on their sweaty backs. And in turn, there were louder complaints and threats against me.

Seeing how much harder the people had to work, I prayed, *Oh, God, please have mercy on your people! Pharaoh has refused to let the Israelites go and has made things only worse. He has made their labors harder! Where is their rescue? When is their salvation? What do You want me to do? Lord, why did You send me to Pharaoh?*

The Lord said, *Watch now, and you will see My work and what I will do to Pharaoh and the worthless gods of Egypt. In the end, Pharaoh will be glad to see My children go, and will even drive them out from Egypt with a strong arm! Tell the Israelites that I have heard their groaning and seen their oppression.*

As expected, the Israelites didn't listen to me or believe I had heard the promise from God. They continued to blame me for their increased workload and cruel bondage! It seemed that the waves of their troubled lives now turned into fierce whitecaps threatening to destroy them. Not only did I feel that my life was in jeopardy at the courts of Pharaoh, but it was also in danger at the hands of the Israelites.

Then the Lord said to me, *Return to Pharaoh. Do not request of him to let My people go, but tell him to let My people go!*

Lord, Your own people don't believe me, so how can I, with my halting speech, convince Pharaoh? Please, Lord, he won't listen to me and may even deny an audience with him. You saw how Aaron and I were roughly removed from the palace even at sword point.

Because of my awkward speech, God again reminded me, *I will tell you what to say through Aaron. He will again repeat your words and commands to Pharaoh.*

Then again, God reminded me that He would harden Pharaoh's heart so that He could perform many miraculous wonders and terrible plagues on Egypt before Pharaoh would finally let the Israelites go.

I wondered why God said He would *harden* Pharaoh's heart. If Pharaoh's heart were "hardened," and he refused to let the Israelites leave, was God planning to *destroy* Pharaoh and Egypt with multiple disasters? What would finally persuade this proud king to let God's people go and "drive them from Egypt?" Perhaps the "hardening" was simply the withdrawal of God's Spirit—the Spirit that draws and influences man *toward* God.

While living in Midian, I understood the Holy Spirit's influence and the drawing of myself to God. In any case, whatever was in God's plan, I was told that Pharaoh's heart would be "hardened." I just had to believe and trust in God—the great I AM.

Thutmose III

FROM HAUGHTY TO HUMBLE

M.J. FERGUSON

URAEUS
PROTECTOR of EGYPT

Uraeus, the Cobra God

The Egyptians have several serpent gods. Uraeus was the cobra god, the protector of Egypt, and was worn on the headdress of the Pharaohs. But the strongest and the one most feared was Apep, who was believed to be in constant conflict with Ra, the sun god.

At God's command, Aaron and I went back to Pharaoh—alone this time, without the Elders. Again, I stood boldly and looked straight into the eyes of this haughty tyrant with the confidence given to me by God! I spoke directly to this king in the Hebrew language, which Aaron translated into Egyptian.

"The God of our fathers, the great IAM says, 'Let My people go!'"

With a glare from his raven eyes, he said, "Let My people go? I have already told you those Hebrew slaves belong to *me*, and they cannot leave! What gives you the right to make such an absurd demand? Show me your authority and your God! Show me some miracle, some power, some proof that I should grant your claim to my property."

Aaron then threw down his staff, and it became a snake—a venomous and threatening viper. Those standing nearby quickly backed away, but the sorcerers and magicians just laughed and did the same with their staffs. The laughing stopped, however, when Aaron's snake ate theirs!

After Aaron picked up the snake by the tail, it turned back into his staff.

Pharaoh gazed at me with caution and seemed to regard me as some sort of deity—a god. Otherwise, this powerful Pharaoh, Thutmose III, could have easily ordered our deaths. He said nothing but pointed to the entrance of the throne room. We were again ushered out by the guards but this time by sword point only. They did not brutally grab our arms as they had done before—perhaps out of fear or respect to us.

M.J. FERGUSON

HAPI GOD of NILE

BLOOD

The First Plague: Blood

Hapi, the god of the Nile, was worshiped by the Egyptians as a water life source for their drinking, their crops, and their animals. *Hapi* was both male and female and blue in color. Lotus flowers were worn on his/her head, and bread was carried and provided for the Egyptians. When the Nile River turned to blood, it was a direct dispute against this powerless god to save the fish and provide drinking water for the people and their animals. Note that Hapi and most of the gods carried an "ankh" (a ring with a cross) that was the sign of power and life. Most of the gods also carried a scepter called a "was" that indicated divine power.

God told me to go to the Nile River early the next morning and wait for Pharaoh. He and his priests would be arriving to pay homage to Hapi, the Nile god. We were met with suspicion, and they took issue with us about our boldness. Spears were pointed at us. This was the third time Pharaoh and I were face-to-face, but he looked on me as no more than a nuisance—a troublesome vermin.

Aaron said, "You have not listened and have refused to let the Hebrews go to worship their God. Because you have not complied, when my staff touches the Nile, the water will turn to blood, and the fish will die."

With a sarcastic guffaw, this proud king turned his back to us and walked up the marble steps from the river to a shaded throne. When the tip of Aaron's rod touched the water, a gasp of horror was heard from the priests as blood was quickly and eerily spreading across the Nile River. Blood was in *all* their water—their cisterns, their holy vessels, and their wells. Fish started floating to the surface and, along with them, an appalling stench. The blood in the Nile went even as far north as Goshen but to a much lesser degree. For the next several days, the Egyptians had to dig new wells for drinking water for themselves and for their animals.

HEKET

GODDESS of FERTILITY

FROGS

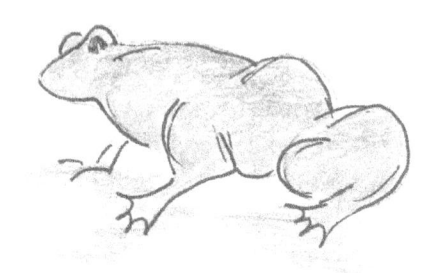

The Second Plague: Frogs

The Egyptians worshipped *Heket*, who was the goddess of fertility. She was usually depicted as a frog or a woman with the head of a frog, and she was green.

After several days, God told me to go to Pharaoh again and say, "If you still refuse to let God's people go, He will send frogs out of the Nile. They will cover the land and invade your homes."

Frogs were considered sacred by Egyptians, and the people were forbidden to kill or harm them. Now, the frogs were everywhere! They were in their homes, their beds, and in their bread-making bowls.

Pharaoh sent a message for me to come to the palace. Upon arrival, I cautiously walked into his throne room, carefully trying to avoid stepping on any *frogs*. They were everywhere, a really disgusting sight. I did not bow. I waited for him to speak first. There were servants constantly trying to keep the frogs off the raised dais. Before speaking, he casually brushed a frog off the arm of his throne, which made me smile. *He* wasn't smiling!

"Ah, Moses, get rid of these frogs!"

"Yes, Sire. When do you want me to pray to *my* God to remove them?"

"Tomorrow! Tomorrow!" he yelled. "*Then* I will let your people go."

Tomorrow? Why didn't Pharaoh want the frogs removed this same day? Did he think that they would go away on their own, and then he wouldn't have to acknowledge the power of the only true God? Oh, foolish king!

So the next day, I prayed to the Lord, and all the frogs died that were in the houses and that covered the land. The dead frogs were collected into great heaps, and the whole land reeked with the stench, which was worse than the smell of the dead fish from the bloody Nile River. Pharaoh hardened his heart again and refused to let the people go.

M.J. FERGUSON

GEB GOD of EARTH

LICE/FLEAS

The Third Plague: Fleas/Lice

Geb was the Egyptian god of the earth and was usually depicted as reclining, which indicated mountains and valleys. He was dark in color and covered with leaves and vegetation.

Since the frogs were dead and buried, and the Nile River was flowing now with fresh water, Pharaoh had no intention of keeping his word of letting his slaves leave Egypt. He denied the promise he made. At this announcement, I invited this king to follow Aaron and me outside. As instructed by the only *true* God, I told Aaron to strike the ground with his staff in the presence of Pharaoh. Amused at the small puff of dust caused by Aaron's staff hitting the dirt, this king laughed and turned to walk away.

Suddenly, the dust of the ground began to swirl around and around. Bigger and bigger, it turned until it became a very large "dust devil." Then this dust turned into a plague of lice and fleas that covered all of Egypt. The air was thick with these biting insects that affected both man and beast for several days.

The priests of Geb, who were known for their "purity" with completely shaved bodies and long, white tunics, were unable to keep themselves disinfected for their rituals.

The magicians and sorcerers said to Pharaoh, "We are unable to reproduce this plague as we did the others. And Geb, our god of the earth, will not hear us to move this infestation. This is undoubtedly the hand of *their* powerful God. Can it be that the God of this Moses is stronger than Geb?"

KHEPRI
GOD of RENEWAL/REBIRTH

SCARAB SWARM

The Fourth Plague: Swarms

Khepri was a god of renewal, rebirth, and resurrection. He was depicted as a powerful god with the head of a scarab beetle. The scarab beetle was worshipped and pictured on many walls and tombs in Egypt. It was believed that this beetle caused the sun to rise every morning and pushed it across the sky until evening.

(Note: The King James Bible [Exodus 8:21–31] read seven times that the fourth plague was a "swarm," but the words "of flies" is in italics, which indicate it was added, possibly for a better explanation. Therefore, it may *not* have been a swarm of "flies" but a swarm of flying scarab beetles.)

Then God said to me, *Get up early in the morning and go to Pharaoh. Tell him, "If you will not let My people go, beginning tomorrow, I will send a flying swarm with stinging and painful bites, and they will cover the land. So that you will know that I am God, the only living and powerful God, this plague will not be in Goshen where My people live. You will know that I make a distinction between My people and your people, the Egyptians."*

After the lice and flees were gone, the evidence remained on the bodies of the Egyptians and Pharaoh. They had red bites that caused intense itching, even sickness and fever. With our announcement of the coming flying swarm, those in attendance at the palace looked aghast at one another while trying to avoid their constant scratching.

Without any further words, Aaron and I were escorted from the presence of Pharaoh at his speechless command. There was silence in the throne room except for the sound of our sandals on the marble floors. All eyes followed our exit, even down the steps of the palace and through the gates of the gardens.

God reminded me that he would continue to assert His power over Egypt and their *worthless gods*. Khepri proved to be as worthless as he was repulsive—a man with the head of a beetle! God said He would send plague after plague to destroy their lands and their idols. So evidently, there was more to come!

Up until now, all the plagues were also in Goshen and among the Israelite's slave camps but to a lesser degree than in southern Egypt where Pharaoh's palace stood. As troublesome as these plagues were, God's people saw that their distress was not nearly as intense as the Egyptians'. I had assured them that the coming flying swarm and other plagues would not extend to them, their herds, or their lands.

The flying beetles felt like pebbles being thrown at the bodies of the Egyptians causing bruising and even some bleeding. During this flying swarm, Pharaoh called for Aaron and me.

"Okay, okay! You may worship your God, but *here* in Egypt only! I give permission for the Hebrews to offer sacrifices to their God but only in *Goshen*! They are *not* allowed to leave Egypt!"

"No! That is *not* acceptable!" With boldness, I added, "Our sacrifices are detested and an abomination to the Egyptians, and if they see us making these offerings, they will surely stone us. No! We must go a three-day journey into the wilderness as our God has commanded."

With a red face and clinched jaw, Pharaoh conceded, "Okay, you may go and make your sacrifices, but do *not* go far! *Not* a three-day journey! That is my consent and command! Now, ask your God to remove these venomous vermin from our land and our homes!"

I promised Pharaoh that I would intercede for him after I left his court but added, "Do not be flippant with your words or amuse yourself with changing your mind. Our God demands respect, even from you, oh King."

Aaron and I left Pharaoh's presence without the usual escort of soldiers or spears. But once again, and through the advice of his councilors, Pharaoh hardened his heart. He refused to release the Israelites.

FROM HAUGHTY TO HUMBLE

HATHOR

GODDESS of LOVE & PROTECTION

CATTLE DEATH

The Fifth Plague: Livestock Death

Pharaoh and his courtiers prayed to *Hathor*, the goddess of love and protection, who had the head or horns of a cow. This goddess was very popular in Egypt. There were numerous festivals in her honor, and many children were named after this goddess. *Apis* was another god of cattle. Since there were hundreds of Egyptian gods, many had common roles and missions, either for protection or punishment of the people.

Again, I was instructed by God to stand before Pharaoh.

"These are God's words, 'If you do not let My people go, I will strike your herds, your sacred animals, and your beasts of burden with a fatal disease. Many of your oxen, horses, camels, donkeys, and sheep will die.'"

So far, the plagues caused only discomfort to Pharaoh and the Egyptians, but the death of their livestock would bring a huge economic disaster to their nation. At the announcement of this coming curse, Pharaoh's face was visibly distraught.

He stood up and shouted, "And when will this happen?"

"Tomorrow! But know this, *none* of the animals in Goshen will be killed."

Surely, *this* terrible plague would soften Pharaoh's heart, and he would let the Israelites leave Egypt.

The very next day, a vast number of the Egyptian livestock died. Their goddess, *Hathor*, and the other gods they prayed to were unable to shield or save them. After sending an inquiry to Goshen, Pharaoh was told that *none* of the Hebrews' cattle had died. That made him furious! And yet upon the advice of his counselors, he remained stubborn and refused to let God's people go.

M.J. FERGUSON

ISIS GODDESS of HEALTH & HEALING

BOILS

The Sixth Plague: Boils

All of Egypt saw the folly of their priests who pleaded and gyrated in front of their gods of health and healing. Among these gods were *Isis*, *Sekhmet*, and *Imhotep*. Imhotep had previously been a man but became a god of healing after his death.

I was then instructed by God to return to Pharaoh with the news of *another* plague. This time, I just stood silent before Pharaoh and his counselors. It was not a peaceful silence. It was filled to the brim with deafening tension. As always, I looked directly into his angry eyes. I said nothing. The suspense was heavy throughout the throne room. After looking for several long moments into this king's furious ebony stare, I turned and walked to a furnace filled with cooled ashes. With both my hands, I scooped up the gray-white powdery residue and walked toward the balcony. Without either of us speaking, Pharaoh stood up from his throne and followed me to the balcony of his palace. All was quiet except for the footsteps echoing off the marble walls.

With my eyes closed and face toward heaven, I whispered a quiet prayer and threw the ashes into the gentle warm breeze, which carried them over the land of Egypt, the people, and the animals. The white powder swirled like a small vortex in the throne room. As Aaron and I left the palace without saying a word, there were a few muffled snickers, but mostly, there was silence. No threats, no laughing, no angry responses—just silence. *Deadly silence*!

The priests, magicians, and sorcerers had always encouraged Pharaoh, saying, "You must resist this mad man, Moses, and his God. You cannot let the Hebrews leave Egypt." But when painful boils broke out on their own bodies, they had no words of defiance. Boils festered on man and beast, from Pharaoh to the lowest servant and to the beasts of burden. There was constant pain from the miserable and draining boils! The putrid pustules on Pharaoh did not soften his heart but made him angrier and more defiant.

M.J. FERGUSON

NUT GODDESS of SKY

HAIL

The Seventh Plague: Hail

Nut was the goddess of the sky and the mother of many other Egyptian gods. She was depicted as arching over the earth in a protective manner. She was blue in color and covered with stars.

About a week later, I boldly returned to Pharaoh's court. This proud and arrogant king looked terrible with pathetic yellow poultices plastered on his face, arms, and legs. Sitting on his throne, he barely acknowledged my presence.

Through Aaron, I told this haughty monarch, "If you do not let God's people go to worship Him, He will strike yet another plague on you and your lands so that you will know that there is none like Him. Be aware, oh King, our God could have easily destroyed you and *vanished* you from the earth! But you have been allowed to live only to show His power to all of Egypt and the *rest of the world*. So if you do not let His people go by tomorrow, He will send hail such as Egypt has never seen before." Adding a warning, I then advised, "Bring all that is left of your herds, horses, and servants out of the fields into buildings for protection or they too will be destroyed. Your revered goddess of the sky, *Nut*, will prove to you and all of Egypt to be *worthless*. You will know that *my* God has control of even the sky, and in Him only is there safety and protection."

Pharaoh made no comment and no threats. He just rolled his bloodshot eyes and looked at me with stoical indifference. We turned and walked out, again without an escort of soldiers or guards.

All the previous plagues caused misery and discomfort for the Egyptians, but this latest plague promised death to more of their herds and any servants in the fields that were not under adequate cover. This hail was severe, a phenomenon unknown to Egypt, bringing death to herds and servants and destruction to crops and trees. Even some of the lesser buildings were broken to pieces.

Aaron and I always went to Pharaoh at God's command. But *during* this plague of hail, Pharaoh *sent* for us! After seven terrible plagues of pain and death, I thought perhaps this plague of hail was probably the last. Surely, Pharaoh would now drive the Israelites from this country as God had promised he would.

When we arrived at the palace, he bellowed in resignation, "Enough! Enough, Moses! I and my people have sinned against your God. We cannot take anymore! Ask your God to stop this devastation, and I will let your people go."

I promised Pharaoh I would pray to the *only true* God to stop the hail as soon as we were out of the city. The king and his courtiers curiously watched as Aaron and I walked without fear through the hailstorm obviously protected!

Certainly, this king would *now* keep his word or Egypt would be completely destroyed. Already, most of their herds were dead. Their fields, trees, and many buildings were ruined. However, their prized horses had been protected in their durable stables.

In my prayer, God said to me, *I will again harden Pharaoh's heart. More plagues are to come. The events happening now in Egypt will be told throughout the world for many generations. The devastation will be witnessed by My children, but they will not be harmed in any way. My protection will strengthen their faith in Me and give them hope for their deliverance. I AM the only true God.*

M.J. FERGUSON

NEPRI
GOD of GRAIN & FIELDS

LOCUST

The Eighth Plague: Locust

Nepri was the god of grain, who created Egypt's wealth. Grain was often used in trade instead of money. *Shu* was the god of the atmosphere and of all of the space between the ground and sky.

After the hailstorm, and after Pharaoh's heart was hardened, God told me to return with another warning of more destruction to come.

As Aaron and I walked into Pharaoh's presence, only the *pretense* of dignity was evident. After each plague, the previously pristine polish and shine of the throne room took on a dusty and distressed appearance. His counselors looked ashen and gaunt with traces of healing boils still on their faces and arms.

"Hear me, oh, Pharaoh. Because of your stubbornness, God will send a plague of locust to cover the land. They will eat up every green thing that the hail did not destroy. Nothing will remain, and your people will starve!"

Pharaoh just glared at me, but his counselors appeared horror-struck. They were speechless as they glanced around the throne room at each other.

They seemed to understand the difficulty of a nation surviving without food, cattle, or any resources for rebuilding.

Finally, one of them said, "Oh, Pharaoh, Son of Ra, how long do we have to tolerate this man? Let the Hebrew slaves go and worship their God. Get them out of here or we will all be completely destroyed! Egypt cannot take another curse from *their God!*"

In a huff, and with his fists pounding on the armrests of his throne, Pharaoh replied, "Okay, you can go! But I need to know *who* will be going. It can be *only* you and your elders!"

"No! *Everyone* will go! Our men, our women, our young, and our old!"

Now standing and screaming, he said, "No! I *cannot* allow that! *I will not! Only* your men may go! Take it or leave it!"

With that *weak* compromise from the ruler of a crumbling nation, there was no more discussion. Pharaoh then pointed to his hardened guards indicating that Aaron and I were to be driven out of the palace at once. A couple of guards, with evidence of healing boils still on their faces, hung back in apparent fear of the God who had proven to be stronger than their idols.

After leaving the city, I stretched my rod over the land. A strong east wind began to blow that brought locusts, which covered and darkened the ground. Every green plant was devoured. Egypt was wiped clean of all vegetation. The only food that had not been destroyed by this vermin was the grain in the storehouses.

How much longer, oh, God? What will make Pharaoh change his mind and let Your people go, and "drive" them out of Egypt?

Pharaoh sent for me again. Aaron and I walked into the once-beautiful throne room. Live and dead locust covered the marble floors. What a sight and what a terrible sound of *crunching* as we took every step.

With his back to me, Pharaoh said, "Moses, I have sinned against your God. I have sinned against my people. They are afraid for our future, and they distrust the power of *our* gods. I have personally pleaded with *Shu* and *Nepri* to rid us of these ravenous locusts. Yet still they remain!"

Finally turning slowly to face me, he *almost* humbly added with a shrug, and his arm outstretched, "What is left for them to eat? And now, my people even doubt that *I, the Son of Ra,* am a god! Now, please, another time, ask your God to remove His curse against Egypt."

Without a bow or even a nod, I walked to the balcony, and I raised my staff again over the land, and God caused a strong *west* wind to blow the locusts out to the sea. The locusts were gone and so was all vegetation. Egypt was swept clean of any growing or green thing—even the potted plants that decorated the palace were devoured down to the dirt!

The children of Israel watched Egypt being destroyed by the hand of God. They saw the years of their hard labor wiped away in a matter of weeks because of the stubbornness of Pharaoh. Yet their lands were untouched by the judgments of God. They were becoming confident that their liberation was near.

The Egyptians also saw the difference between their country and the lands in Goshen. Many of them felt they might be saved if they could somehow find favor with the Hebrews. They brought many gifts of gold and silver. They brought earrings, jewelry, pearls, diamonds, and precious stones. They brought fine linens, silk, and camel skins. All these gifts were an attempt to build an alliance with the Hebrews and gain their approval and support. Any request by a Hebrew for an object, or a favor, was quickly granted by many of the Egyptians.

FROM HAUGHTY TO HUMBLE

RA SUN GOD

DARKNESS

The Ninth Plague: Darkness

Ra was the sun god and considered the most powerful of all the gods of Egypt. He was depicted with the body of a man and the head of a hawk with the sun disk on top of his head. Pharaoh, himself, was the son of *Ra* and, therefore, also a sun god.

After the locusts were gone, God told me to stretch out my hand toward the sky. Suddenly, there was darkness, and it covered the land for three days. It was thick and murky and could actually be *felt*. Its heaviness was like a black fog that made it hard to breathe! Exceedingly oppressive! Fire or lamps could not penetrate this shroud. This curse was in direct conflict with *Ra*, the sun god, and proved that the true God of the Israelites was ruler, *even of the sun*. The Egyptians saw that Pharaoh, their sun god, was impotent over the all-powerful God of the Hebrews.

After the three days of the oppressive and murky blackness, many Egyptians were sick with respiratory disorders—coughing, wheezing, and choking! For almost thirty years, I had lived in the palace of Pharaoh and among the Egyptians. I was considered one of them, was treated with respect, and honored as the Prince of Egypt. It saddened me to see my old friends suffer because of Pharaoh's stubbornness and defiance to God's command. I felt sympathy toward my Egyptian brothers.

Pharaoh summoned me and said in a raspy voice, "Moses…*every* Hebrew may go to worship their God as He has commanded. All may go *except* your flocks and herds. This way, I will know they will return. For if they don't return, who will rebuild my kingdom for me?"

This time, I spoke *directly* to Pharaoh in the Egyptian language. My response to him was not weak or hesitant.

"No! Everyone will go. We will go with *all* of our flocks and herds. Not even one hoof will be left behind!"

This made Pharaoh furious! His anger, his croaking voice, and his *attempt* at yelling were out of control. He picked up a heavy and worthless idol and threw it across the room, smashing it to pieces against a fire stanchion. This reminded me of forty years ago when Hatshepsut, another powerful Pharaoh, threw a heavy object at my head. Both of them had *hate* in their eyes.

Why? This king must surely realize that he is in a losing battle against the most high God, but he will not admit it or change his mind. He is destroying his whole empire with his stubbornness and pride.

In Pharaoh's rage and raspy cough, he bellowed, "Moses, I *know* who you are! You think I don't know? If you hadn't renounced your right to this throne, you would be Pharaoh of all Egypt instead of me. Your own mother, Hatshepsut, swore to have you killed for turning against her and your Egyptian brothers. But you ran! Run again, Moses! Run from me! Get out of here! I swear by all the gods of Egypt if I see your face again, I will kill you and carry out your death sentence *myself*."

"You are correct, oh King. You will not see my face again!"

I fully realized that Pharaoh could have, at any time, ordered my death over the last many weeks, but God caused the court officials to fear and hold me in high regard. It was evident to all Egyptians that the Great I AM was more powerful than any king or the multitude of gods they worship. God was our protector.

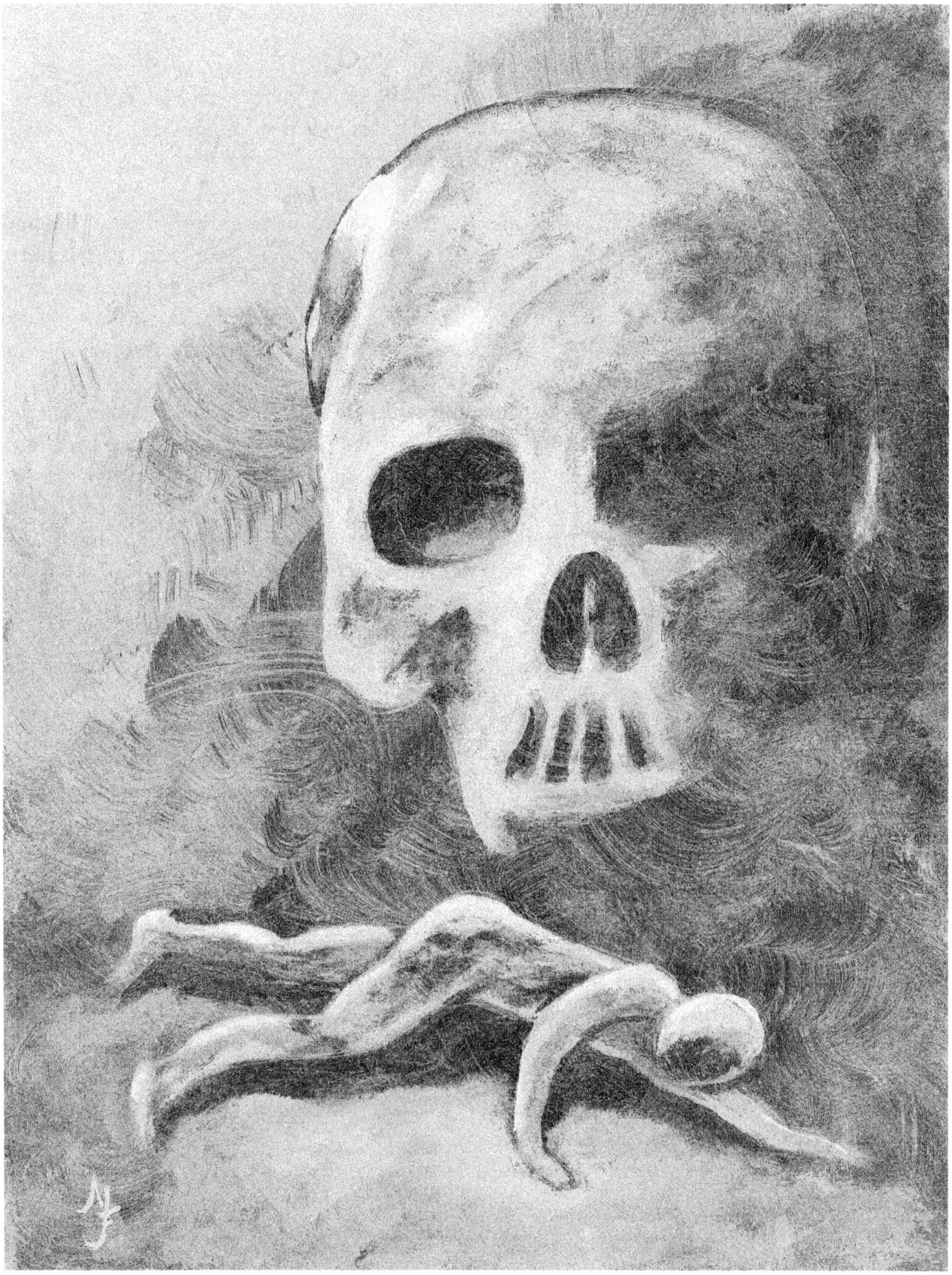

The Tenth Plague: Death Pronouncement

Thutmose III, Pharaoh of Egypt and the son of *Ra*, would experience, firsthand, the pain of losing his firstborn son.

After I left the raging Egyptian monarch, God told me to return with *one last warning*. Again, I spoke directly to Pharaoh in the Egyptian language, man to man, state to state, and power to power.

"Oh, Pharaoh, king of Egypt, hear and take warning of this *last* word from the Lord. On the fourteenth day of this month at around midnight, God will descend onto Egypt, and all the firstborn in the land will die! *Every* firstborn, even *your* firstborn, Amenemhat, who is the Crown Prince of Egypt, will die. All the firstborn of royalty, even to the firstborn of the servants in the mills, will die. Also, the firstborn of your remaining beasts including your magnificent horses will die. There will be great crying and anguish throughout the land…more than was seen after all the other afflictions. So that you will know that God makes a distinction between Egyptians and Israelites, *none* of the Hebrew firstborn will die."

While this terrible pronouncement was contemplated, and before Pharaoh had opportunity to respond with an obscene oath, I added, "After that, oh King, you will let all of God's people leave Egypt! In fact, you will drive them away with your strong arm!"

Pharaoh was visibly shaken and extremely hot with rage. His whole body was filled with hate as he yelled that he would kill *all* the firstborn Israelites if just *one* Egyptian died. Aaron and I turned and left the palace of this king—this Pharaoh of the nearly destroyed period of the eighteenth dynasty.

Pharaoh, Thutmose III, the king of Egypt and monarch of the most powerful nation of the world, was considered a god and was therefore worshipped. This tenth and last plague was a *direct assault against his sovereign rule*.

CHAPTER 13

DEATH OF FIRSTBORN

In preparation for their liberation from Egypt, the Israelites had organized themselves and appointed leaders among the different tribes. They had already obtained the mummified body of Joseph, the eleventh son of Jacob, to take with them. They also acquired much wealth from the Egyptians, which included gold, silver, bronze, iron, rich fabrics, furs, carts, wagons, and tents. None of their requests for Egyptian riches or treasures were denied. Even back pay for years of servitude was granted to the Israelites.

Now, there was much to do in preparing the Israelites for the coming judgment of God to kill all the firstborn of the land—of which they were *not* exempt. Calling together the leaders, I gave them strict and detailed instructions from God on how to avoid the death of their firstborn and about their departure from this land of idolatry and slavery. They were to relay these directives from slave camp to slave camp along the Nile and encourage the Israelites to leave their quarters and move to Goshen in preparation for the Exodus! (My brother's family, along with several other families, stayed in our slave quarters near Thebes.)

God said, *On the tenth day of this month, every household is to select a perfect lamb and tenderly care for it in your homes until the fourteenth day. Smaller households may join with their neighbors to share the expense and duties of this task. At dusk, on the fourteenth day, you are to kill the innocent lamb and sprinkle its blood on your door posts with hyssop. When the angel of death sees the blood, he will not enter your house. He will pass over and will not kill any of your firstborn. Roast the whole lamb over a fire. At midnight, eat the roasted lamb with unleavened bread and bitter herbs. Be dressed and ready to leave Egypt, but do not step outside your homes until the signal is given. Any of the meat that is left must be put in the fire.*

I knew the Hebrew's knowledge and faith in Jehovah was weak and tenuous. But I prayed that seeing the hand of God against their oppressors was enough to give them courage and conviction to follow these lifesaving instructions.

At dusk on the appointed day, there were tears shed, especially by the children, as their chosen and cherished lambs were killed outside their doors, and their blood was collected in bowls. This precious blood was spread on the sides and tops of their doorposts using hyssop as was instructed by God.

FROM HAUGHTY TO HUMBLE

The appointed night was solemn and quiet. The air was still and had no breeze. In silence, parents clung to their children and each other while eating the roasted lamb and unleavened bread. The only sound was the crackling fire and an occasional barking of a dog in the night. My sister, my brother and family, and my aged father shared their home with me and one other family. I knew that this was the *last* and the *most terrible* of the plagues against Pharaoh. God said Pharaoh would drive the Israelites with his strong hand, but I did *not* know when or how.

Then suddenly, with what sounded like a terrible explosion, several Egyptian soldiers *kicked* open our door and demanded that Aaron and I come with them. Pharaoh had ordered our presence, and we were driven on chariots through our quiet and dark streets to the palace. As we got closer, we heard the wailing and crying over the Egyptians' dead firstborn.

We entered the darkened palace that had only one oil lamp burning, casting ominous shadows around the throne room. Pharaoh was alone—no guards, no counselors, and no servants. No pomp, no power, no show of grandeur! This room that looked majestic in riches and power a few months ago now took on the appearance of an abandoned ship with its captain alone and beaten by a storm—dull, dirty, and showing the effects of mutiny.

Pharaoh was stripped to the waist, and standing in front of his throne. No gold, no rings, and no symbols of his royal status as the king of Egypt. He looked ashen, defeated, and much older than his years. At his bare feet, the young man, who was the "Overseer of the Cattle" and Crown Prince of Egypt, Amenemhat, was dead! All of Pharaoh's priests, guards, and gods could not protect his firstborn son.

Since this Pharaoh, Thutmose III, was the *second* child and *only son* of Thutmose II by a secondary wife, Iset, his life was spared. Pharaoh's second son, Amenhotep II, would become the next Pharaoh, king of Egypt. An inheritance of a stripped and desolate nation.

While waiting for Pharaoh to speak, he and I just *looked* at each other for a long time. I could not help feeling sorry for this strong and proud monarch. There was nothing left of him but trembling rage—a hate that came boiling out of his mouth. Finally, with a vile oath against *his* gods, he demanded that all of the Israelites had to leave *this very night*.

Pointing at me, he yelled, "Get out…all of you! You and your God have devastated me, my people, and my nation! Leave me! Take *all* of your retched people and your filthy animals with you! Now that I am defeated and broken, I give you my *permission* to leave."

Give you my permission? Does this Pharaoh think he has any other choice? Does he now realize how pointless his bargains and threats were? This king looks as powerless and worthless as his gods of stone.

Then with a bowed head and slumped shoulders, he sat down on his throne. Without looking directly at me, and in a subdued voice, he meekly said, "Moses, one more thing. Ask your God to bless me."

Bless Pharaoh? It seemed blasphemous to ask God to bless this hardened and cruel king. I felt if God wanted to bless Pharaoh, that was His prerogative, but I would not ask for such a blessing. I would, however, pray for mercy toward him. He was, after all, just a man—not a god. A broken and defeated man!

Pharaoh the Defeated

CHAPTER 14

THE EXODUS

At the predawn light, and at the command from Pharaoh that *all* the Israelites were to "leave this very night," soldiers on their chariots rode through the narrow streets of the mostly abandoned slave camps, shouting and blowing horns to awaken the silent Hebrews who were waiting for the signal—the "all clear" to leave Egypt. Instantly, everyone was ready and knew what to do as had been prearranged by the elder leaders.

With the clamor of many chariots, and soldiers yelling for the evacuation of the Israelites, a shout of joy spread throughout the land. Bags had already been packed with ample food and jugs of water for themselves and their animals. The Israelites were leaving Egypt a wealthy nation, wealth provided to them by their defeated taskmasters. They were leaving with riches, including back pay for their years of cruel servitude. Egypt now lay plundered, stripped, and conquered by the Great I AM.

After all the Israelites had gathered in Goshen from the slave camps, a bright pillar of fire shone in the predawn sky to lead and light the way. Now, six hundred thousand men, plus women and children, including a massive number of animals (sheep, goats, cattle, horses, and camels) were waiting for the signal for the *Exodus*! Among these were many Egyptians who left their homes to join the Israelites. After seeing the power of the Hebrew God, and the impotence of their own worthless deities, some Egyptians abandoned their false gods and gave their hearts to Jehovah. Some, however, just considered it prudent to be connected to the "winning side."

Let My people go! Those words kept running through my head. *Yes, we are going! Thinking back over the past few months, I am certain that Jehovah is in control and that we must follow His light.*

The excitement! The chaos! The clamor from the people, the many carts, and animals sounded like confusion—even war. Now standing in front of this multitude of former slaves, and leading them out of the most powerful nation of the world, seemed a daunting task. Moving this slow and massive population with their children, herds, and possessions would be a formidable responsibility for a man—*any man*! Only God, the King of the universe, could do such a thing!

Oh, God! Who am I to lead these people? Who am I to stand as Your representative? They have seen great and marvelous things against the Egyptians, their oppressors, but their faith is weak. They are mere babes in their knowledge of You, the Great I AM. So much have they forgotten since the time of their father, Jacob.

In the early morning light, when I raised my staff, a shout of excitement and eagerness came in waves from this new and wealthy nation. They were moving away from the only homes they had known all their lives. Yes, their homes were small, but this lower Egypt was a land of green fields fed by the richness and abundance of the Nile River. It was the best land in Egypt given to Joseph's descendants by the Pharaoh more than four hundred years ago. What did they know of anything outside Goshen or the slave camps along the Nile and around the capital city of Pharaoh? In their excitement, they were happy to be leaving their bondage to a cruel king and traveling to Canaan, the land of "milk and honey."

In the morning sun, the presence of God changed from a pillar of fire to a large cloud pillar that began to move slowly and southeastward. *South and eastward? Canaan was north of us!* But then so were the Philistines in the north, and they were a powerful warlike nation. I realized that the Hebrews were not equipped for fighting, neither were they trusting enough in Jehovah to face the mighty Philistines. So instead of heading north to Canaan, we were directed eastward and would be entering the Promised Land by a different route. Then I remembered God telling me that His people would worship Him on "this mountain," which was in Midian of Arabia, a long way from Canaan. Yes, this was the beginning of an extensive and awesome journey, but the Great I AM was leading and in control.

As the sun rose higher in the cloudless sky, the cloud provided shade from the burning heat of the desert. Stopping at night for rest, the cloud became a pillar of fire to provide light and warmth. Both of these were constant reminders of God's mercy. He was leading and protecting us! A thrilling concept!

I had traveled over these rocky deserts many months before, and I wondered how this large throng of people with their carts and massive herds would be able to move without loss or injury. These are desolate and dangerous lands with many hazards. Scorpions, poisonous snakes, sharp rocks, and thorns, to say nothing of boredom and dehydration. All the rocks started looking the same—same color, different size. But our spirits remained high, and God seemed to diminish the common and dangerous desert obstacles.

Oh, God, thank you for your promises and your deliverance from the four hundred years in Egypt. Your people are many, and their faith is fragile. I pray that you will strengthen their faith and have mercy on us.

Chapter 15

The Red Sea

After *many* days of seemingly endless walking during the day and stopping only at night to rest and sleep, the people began to complain.

"Where are you taking us, Moses? Where is this 'Promised Land' we have heard so much about? How much farther?"

"Only God knows. Take courage, and have faith in the God of your fathers. He is leading us where we need to go."

Finally, our second prolonged encampment was a much-needed rest on the large sandy shores of the Aqaba, the northeaster's gulf of the Red Sea. The soft sand was a wonderful relief from the rocks of the dried riverbed we had been traveling on. The delightful breeze coming off the sea was refreshing. Children ran to play in the cooling waters, while many adults enjoyed its refreshing waters too. It was a beautiful resting place, but it was also *impassable* for any further travel. The Gulf of Aqaba, an extension of the Red Sea, was directly in front of us. There were high mountains to the south, high mountains and Philistines to the north, and Egyptians to the west. It appeared we were cornered! Trapped!

Before the delegation of angry men approached, I was expecting their outrage and confrontation.

"Where to now, Moses? Is this the 'Promised Land'? There is obviously no place else for us to go! What will we do when we run out of food and water, Moses? We can't eat sand or grow crops in sand and salt water!"

I tried to assure these irate men that the Lord had taken care of us so far.

"God has a plan, a plan for us... *His* children!"

What that "plan" was, I truthfully did not know.

Where now, oh, Lord? Where do we go from here?

Then God said to me, *Moses, a report has been given to Pharaoh that the Israelites are camped, and cornered here, by the Red Sea. He and his counselors have regretted the decision to let their slaves leave Egypt and are fearful that they won't be returning. They are now claiming that all the plagues that fell on them were of natural causes and have already denied My power. With bitter cries, they have said, "Why did we let those people go? Who will serve us and build up our strength? Other nations will now see our weakness and conquer us." Therefore, Pharaoh has determined to capture and return his fugitives by force.*

He has built a mighty Army with many chariots, horsemen, soldiers, and priests. But do not fear, Moses! I will again demonstrate My power, and bring a final conclusion to Pharaoh's threat. He will no longer be a danger to My people!

After the Lord spoke to me, I looked up and saw a large dust cloud in the distant west and knew immediately it was Pharaoh's Army. As it drew closer, others also saw the evidence of many horses, chariots, and flashes of their metal shields coming toward us. In their fear and panic, they blamed me for bringing them to their deaths.

"Look! Pharaoh and his Army are coming for us! Why have you brought us here? We have been tricked! Were there not any graves in Egypt that we should now die in the *desert*? Didn't we tell you to leave us alone that we may serve the Egyptians? We are cornered! Trapped! There is no escape!"

In their hysteria, violence and panic broke out causing injury and pain to many. It appeared they didn't need the Egyptians to cause affliction. They were doing it among *themselves*!

It saddens me to see how little faith these people have. Hadn't they seen the great devastation of Egypt by the hand of God? Can't they now see the presence of God in the pillar of fire at night and the cooling cloud leading them by day? Oh…such little faith!

"Don't be afraid!" I cried out above the noise of the panicking crowd. "Be still and watch! God will fight for you! The Egyptian Army will be destroyed, and you will never see them again!"

Following God's command, I stood next to the sea and waved my staff over the water. *All that night*, a strong and severe east wind blew, which divided the sea, and a dense cloud of darkness settled over the approaching Egyptian Army, causing disorder and confusion among them. Through the power of our God, the wind made a very wide passage of dry land with a wall of water to the north and a wall of water to the south. During that night of wind, God's presence in the pillar began to move over the dry land of the Red Sea. Now, this waterless and dry sandy riverbed was wide enough for about two million people plus herds and cattle to cross in safety.

Slowly and cautiously at first, the Israelites followed Aaron and me down the slopes of the Red Sea. What a thrilling experience! Yes, the riverbed was *dry*! It was like walking on the desert sand. Then singing, shouting, and laughing broke out as the people realized their escape from the Egyptians was *through* the Red Sea. People, animals, carts! It was like a massive and wealthy nation on the move again. To a new country—Arabia!

In the early morning hours, as the last of the Israelites climbed the bank of the shore to safety, God lifted the dark cloud surrounding the Egyptian Army. In Pharaoh's determination to retrieve the fugitives, he ordered his Army onto the dry seabed while he stayed on the western shore. The Egyptian soldiers were in fast pursuit when some of their chariot wheels began falling off. Horses panicked when the cloud over the sea sent out lightning and torrential rain. The thunder shook the sandy river bottom, and it was turning marshy from the downpour. There was no control or leadership of the soldiers on horseback or chariots. Confusion and fear prevailed, and many began turning back. No discipline—just chaos and panic, as they tried to save themselves for fear that the walls of water would close in on them.

Fear struck the hearts of the Israelites as they saw the Egyptian soldiers coming after them. Fear again? Yes, again!

FROM HAUGHTY TO HUMBLE

I don't understand these people. They have just witnessed a monumental miracle by God, and they are afraid? They still don't trust that God will deliver them?

Early that morning, just after daybreak when all the Israelites were safe on the Arabian shore, God told me to raise my staff; the waters came together with a tremendous force. All the Egyptian soldiers and their horses were caught in the torrent and cascade of water. Broken to pieces and drowned! Not only had Egypt been stripped and plundered of their riches, now Pharaoh's Army, prized horses, and chariots were gone too. Thutmose III left little inheritance for his surviving second son, Amenhotep II.

The breathtaking scene of the dead bodies of men and horses that washed onto the shore caused a hush over the multitude. In their silence, they gave respect and honor to God. Some were kneeling, and some were shedding tears—humbling tears. Tears of thanksgiving, tears of freedom, tears of wonderment and reverence to the God of their deliverance. This event will undoubtedly be etched in their memories forever and told for thousands of generations to come. Eventually, there was a shout of triumph and joyful singing, which was led by my sister, Miriam.

We were now in Arabia and *out of Egypt*, out of Pharaoh's tyranny, out of slavery! It was all behind us! With God's leading, we now had His power and supremacy *for* us, for our children, and all generations to come!

Looking back over the closed and flowing Red Sea, I thought of how far I had come—from a baby hidden from Pharaoh's wrath to the Crowned Prince of Egypt destined to be the next Pharaoh. Through my own pride, I found myself a fugitive with a price on my head. Now through God's leading, I was shepherding His people (a massive nation, rich in Egyptian gold and silver, but weak in faith) to the Promised Land in Canaan.

Lord, give me strength and wisdom. I can't do this alone. Only through your mighty power can this be done.

CHAPTER 16

BITTER WATERS/MANNA BEGINS

Freedom! Arabia! After crossing the Red Sea, we were no longer in the lands ruled by Egypt. No more fear of the Pharaoh and the Egyptians. Our spirits were high as we traveled into the barren desert, stopping only to sleep at night. Three days after crossing the Red Sea, our water supply was getting very low. There was a grumbling that began to spread, subtle and sinister at first. Eventually, the complaining irrupted and spread like a wildfire.

"Water…we need water! Where are we going to find water in this desert, Moses? You have led us to the desert to die! We are all going to die!"

Yes, we were getting low on precious water, but it wasn't completely gone. The carts and wagons had been well stocked with water jugs and food. No one was suffering from thirst or hunger. So far, all of our needs had been met. We were cooled by the Cloud during the day, and warmed and comforted by the Pillar of Fire at night. No one had become crippled or disabled during our long journey. No injuries and no sickness. Only the very old or very young had ridden in the carts or wagons. Singing occasionally had broken out in groups—encouraging themselves and others around them. We were traveling to the "Promised Land."

Upon reaching Marah, there was a great shout of joy, "Water! Water!" as they ran to the cool spring and dipped their faces in the water. But the water was bitter and unfit to drink! Again, with anger and spiteful cries, they turned against me!

Do I know what to do about this bitter water? How quick they are to complain and blame me for their fears and forget the past!

I held up my hand and my staff and prayed to our God, who was a constant and visible presence and Who already knew of our need for water. After asking for God's help, He led me to a small tree.

Cut down the tree, and throw it in the water.

What? Cut it down? With what, Lord?

Some of the grumbling hushed when I got hold of a large sword and began chopping at the base of the tree.

"What is Moses doing?" they asked. "We need good drinking water, not *firewood*."

Bark chips were flying everywhere, and shortly the tree fell. It was easier than I expected it to be. I should have known!

Upon doing as God told me to do, and with the help of a few men, we threw the tree into the spring. I then scooped a handful of water to my mouth and tasted it. All eyes were on me as I broke into a big grin and said one word, "Sweet!" The water was cool, refreshing, and "sweet." A shout of joy rang through the people. Everyone replenished their jugs and waterskins and had their fill. Before moving onward, many of the children splashed in the cool spring while the animals drank what they needed. This was additional evidence that God was watching His people and leading us.

From Marah, we followed the cloud to Elim where there were twelve water wells and seventy palm trees. I had almost forgotten the beauty and the delicious sweet dates of the palm trees in Egypt. Such a delightful sight and special treat! The ground, however, was still barren of enough vegetation for the animals, and many died. After three days, complaining again irrupted into hostility.

"Look, Moses! Some of our herds have died due to lack of food for them. In Egypt, the Nile provided *plenty* of fresh vegetation for our animals and for us. What is going to happen to us and our children? We are afraid for our future! You promised us the land of Canaan, filled with 'milk and honey,' but look at us! We are traveling in the *opposite* direction of Canaan and are probably destined to die of starvation! Some of us are talking about moving our families northward to Canaan or even returning to Egypt."

Yes, some of their animals had died. I didn't know why God allowed that, but perhaps our herds were too large. Perhaps the people trusted unreasonably in the wealth of their flocks. I understood their anxiety, but *please!* They still had food, and no one was suffering from hunger, but they were afraid for the future—*the future!*

God has promised them strength and vigor if they will just trust in Him, but they seem unwilling to believe beyond their present provisions and desires.

How can they forget their bitter bondage in Egypt? How can they forget the plagues inflicted by God upon their oppressors? How can they forget the crossing of the Red Sea and the final destruction of Pharaoh's Army? How can they forget the constant reminder of God's presence in the cloud to shade them from the desert heat…or the pillar of fire to provide light and warmth at night? They exaggerate their inconveniences and amplify their trials, yet no one…no one is suffering!

Leading and protecting Jethro's sheep in the desert not far from here was *nothing* in comparison to leading these people. I was never afraid of the sheep rebelling or *threatening* me. They never bullied me or schemed to move to greener pastures. Occasionally, one of the lambs got lost or hurt. If one was lost, I would hunt for it and bring it back to the fold. As a general in Pharaoh's Army, I would shout my commands, and they would be obeyed! Then as a shepherd for Jethro's herd, I had to learn to speak gently, or they would run away. Such peaceful days, caring for sheep!

Lord, what lessons do You have for me now? What do I need to lead these—Your people?

Humbly, and in shame, I took their complaints and fears of low food supply to God.

God replied, *I will give them meat tonight and bread in the morning. Hear Me now, Moses, and tell them how to collect and care for their bread.*

It always amazed me that these two million people could hear every word I was instructed by God to tell them—a miracle in itself! Standing on higher ground above the multitude, I could be seen and heard by all of them.

"Now hear the reply of our Lord. Tonight, the Great I AM will send you meat to eat. There will be quail enough for everyone. In the morning, He will send bread from heaven. The bread will be in the form of tiny white seeds. It may be eaten raw, boiled for porridge, or ground into flour and baked into cakes. In those early morning hours, you will collect an omer (about three and one-half quarts) for every person in your household, but don't save any for the next day because it will become wormy and rotten. On the sixth morning, collect twice as much for each person because on the seventh day, which is the Sabbath, no bread will be found. The bread collected on the sixth day will not be spoiled for the seventh day—the Sabbath."

After catching, roasting, and eating the quail that God had sent them, many of them were still full in the morning from *gorging* themselves the night before. Early in the morning the next day, while some of the cooking fires were still smoldering, the ground was covered with small frost-looking seeds that were white and shiny.

"What is it?" they asked. "Is this our 'bread' from heaven? It is so tiny, and it tastes like…like wafers made with *honey*."

Many filled their pots with this "manna," while some, still full from the night of overeating of quail meat, thought they would wait until later in the day to gather their *bread*. But before the sun was high in the sky, the manna melted, the same way that frost melts from the heat of the sun. Their "bread" was gone!

They quickly learned to gather their manna early every morning, but still being fearful for the *future*, some saved their bread or cakes for the next day. As was warned by God, their saved bread became filled with worms and had a foul, rotten odor. So terrible was the smell that they had to take it outside the camp to bury it.

When the sixth day arrived with twice as much manna on the ground, as promised, most gathered twice the amount.

Still others, who gathered for only one day, said, "The last time I saved the manna for the next day, it was *rotten*. I won't do *that* again!"

So on the seventh day, the Sabbath, they went out to gather the manna as before, but they found *nothing*. They had nothing to eat unless their neighbors shared what they could with them.

Why…why? Why don't these people follow God's commands?

Even in their disobedience, they grumbled and complained, "It isn't *our* fault. We didn't understand the instructions."

They understood! Believe me, there was *no* misunderstanding! The directive from God was *not* complicated—it was clear, clean, and easy. They deliberately abused their blessing—the "bread from heaven." The food of angels!

It didn't take very long, however, before everyone was in total compliance with the gathering of the manna. Even the children were taught to help. And usually, it was the small ones who were first out their tent doors to eat their fill of the sweetness. More of the sweetness went into their mouths than into their jars!

Cooperation and trust in following God's instructions gave the Israelites peace and synergy. They had food and water for themselves and their animals. Even in this desert, a desert that was normally barren of vegetation and shade trees, God provided fertile grazing for the flocks and herds. He provided ample wood for their cooking fires. There was *nothing* lacking for their needs, and they were content and comfortable. True, it wasn't the "land of milk and honey" of Canaan, but this desert was beautiful with grass and stunning wild flowers. Sweet singing and clapping could be heard around the evening campfires!

CHAPTER 17

WATER FROM THE ROCK

Whenever the cloud began to move, we had trumpeters to sound the alert for the Israelites to take action and prepare to relocate. With excitement, anticipation, and minimal grumbling, everyone again pulled up their tent stakes, gathered all their possessions, packed their bags and carts, and followed the great I AM in the cloud to Rephidim. But there was *no water* there, and the land was barren. As long as food, water, shade, and comfort were provided, the people promised to obey and give thanks to God. But as soon as they felt their future was in question, an undulating alarm rippled throughout the camp, and they again panicked!

In their hysteria, a large group of raging men along with a few women approached me, carrying stones and cudgels. All were shouting and waving their arms furiously. The leader of this mob was tall and bare chested with muscles flexed and shiny from perspiring under the bright sun. He had a stubble beard and very short hair. He was obviously one of the "mixed multitude," a self-appointed, volatile spokesman—an Egyptian!

"I *know* you, Moses! You *pretended* to be an Egyptian and one of us, even the *Prince of Egypt*! But look at you now…an old man living among scorpions and desert rats and promising us a better land. Better than Egypt? Better than the meat and lush gardens of Egypt?"

Looking around at his entourage for encouragement, he added, "Give us water to drink, Moses! Give us water or all of us, including our animals and herds, will die. Why have you brought us here to die of thirst? Is that what you want, Moses? You *want* us to die so you can collect our possessions and make yourself rich! Yes, we know that must be your plan! You want us to die so you can have our gold!"

In all my dealings with Thutmose III, a pharaoh of the most powerful nation, I never truly feared for my life because I was a spokesperson for *God*. I was to lead His people out of Egypt. Now, these people were turning against me *again*! In the past, they complained and *blamed* me for their fears. Some threatened to take their families back to Egypt when they perceived *future* difficulties, but now with clubs and rocks in their hands, their *threats* of killing me were direct and personal.

Oh, God, do these people think eliminating me will give them water? I am standing alone, facing this angry and shouting mob. Uneasiness is now burning in my stomach with the possibility of its sudden irruption. There are no cheerful sounds of birds, no cooling breeze, no support, and no solace. Before me are ruthless jackals and vultures! Standing in front of Pharaoh, it was man against man, power against Power. When I killed an Egyptian and was threatened with death, I ran. Do I run from these angry men and women? They have hate in their eyes and clubs in their hands. Will killing me save them from thirst? I stand alone against this menacing mob. I am old and can't possibly run or hide from them. Please tell me what to do.

I still had trembling in my belly and quaking in my legs, but without any hesitation or stammering in my voice, I was given the courage by God to say, "Why do you dispute with me? Why do you challenge the Lord? Hasn't He supplied all your needs? Hasn't He delivered you from slavery? Hasn't He given you safe passage through the Red Sea and destroyed Pharaoh's Army? Hasn't He given you daily bread and water for you and your herds? Is there any among you who is hungry or thirsty?"

"If God brought us here and supplies our bread, why doesn't He now supply water too? This land is barren. No fresh drinking water. No water or grass for our herds in this useless desert. Is God with us or not? Moses, what will happen to us when our waterskins and jugs are empty? *You* brought us here to die of thirst?"

Lord, what shall I do with these angry people? They are about to stone me! I am an old man standing alone against these raging and violent animals.

Suddenly, there was a low and growing sound of thunder in the cloudless sky, which caused the mob to quiet their threats and back away from me.

Then the Lord said to me, *Take some of the elders with you out of the camp, and you will find a large rock. Strike the rock with your staff, and water will pour out, enough for everyone and their animals.*

With faith in the I AM, several elders and I walked a little distance outside the camp and eventually saw a very tall rock standing alone. We looked at each other and questioningly agreed that this must be "the rock" that would give us water. Not knowing exactly what to expect, I stood off to one side and struck the rock with my staff as instructed by God. A deep rumble reverberated from under the ground. The elders and I looked at each other with tense expectancy. Suddenly, water shot up with such tremendous force that it *split the rock*! This geyser of water got us soaking wet before we could get out of the way. Laughing, we felt like little children splashing one another in a pond. Finally, this powerful tower of water settled into a large gush of lifesaving fullness from between the two halves of the rock. This was not a stream but a "river" for this dry and arid desert.

Again, grass and vegetation began to spring up, providing food for the animals. And as always, there were enough trees for respite shade and wood for our cooking fires. This wilderness was not the barren desert I remembered while traveling between Egypt and Midian. There was real beauty here—grass, flowers, and trees—all provided by God.

Getting settled in our new camp at Rephidim beside the incredible river of fresh water required work and patience. I was hopeful that I would soon see my wife, Zipporah, and sons, Gershom and

Eliezer, again but realized I must wait until the Lord gave me permission to leave. It had been many long months since I left my family living in Jethro's community in Midian.

The Amalekites were a warlike tribe living in this region. They had heard of Egypt's defeat and ridiculed the fear of the surrounding nations toward the Israelites in the wilderness. In their foolishness and pride, they called upon their gods and attacked our camp unprovoked! But through the deliverance of the Great I AM, the only true God, we defeated Amalek's Army.

Chapter 18

Jethro's Advice

We didn't often see travelers in this country, but one day, in the distance, I saw a company of people obviously heading toward us. Some were walking, and some were riding camels. As the group got closer, I began to recognize the leader of the entourage and ran toward him. It was my father-in-law, Jethro, followed by my family and many servants I recognized from my forty years in Midian. What a marvelous reunion! My wife was as beautiful as I remembered, and my sons were strong men with their own families.

I invited everyone into my humble tent and provided them with rest, refreshments, and cool water to wash their tired and dusty feet. My tent was nothing like the tents of Jethro. No plush and colorful pillows, no rich multicolored rugs, no ornate oil lamps, no servants to provide lavish trays of food. Even the cushions we sat on now were borrowed from neighbors! Yet we were comfortable and happy to be sharing time together.

I had so much to tell them about all that God had done to the Egyptians and their worthless gods. I related the hardness of Pharaoh's heart and the destruction of Egypt. I also gave account of the miraculous events of protection given by God for the Israelites and the crossing of the Red Sea. So much to relate! So many blessings!

The next day, I went to my usual seated position at the edge of the camp to hear complaints and make judgments from morning till evening on behalf of the people with grievances expressed between them. They were mostly petty disputes, trifling disagreements, and squabbling. Occasionally, a more serious controversy was brought to me, and I had to make a verdict between the two or more complaining parties.

"What are you doing, Moses?"

Surprised at Jethro's question, I answered, "The people come to me with questions and disputes, and I decide the action to be taken between them. This helps keep harmony and cooperation in the camp. It is vitally necessary for peace and fellowship. Don't you agree?"

"Yes, I agree, but you are wearing yourself out, Moses. You cannot keep doing this all by yourself. Get help! Now, let me give *you* some advice. Select some God-fearing and capable men to help make judgments. The very difficult problems can be brought to you, but the simple cases can be handled between those competent men."

With this wise advice from Jethro, Aaron and a few other elders helped me select judges for the people. We chose men who would officiate over groups of thousands, hundreds, fifties, and tens. The difficult cases would be brought to me.

This counsel from Jethro turned out to be prudent advice. Some days, I had several grievances, and some days, I had none. God gave me the wisdom to make the necessary analyses and judgments.

Jethro was pleased with the efficient plan, and in time, he and most of his servants returned to his own community while some devoted servants stayed to help my wife and me. With my added family members, and my son's wives, we needed more room and more tents! These were generously given to us by Jethro before going back to Midian.

Chapter 19

Mount Sinai/Ten Commandments Spoken

After several months, the cloud pillar began to move slowly. Trumpets sounded again to alert the Israelites to prepare for more travel. Slowly, our vast camp moved with all of our possessions and herds through barren lands and mountain passes until we came to the impressive Mount Sinai—the mountain of God. The existence of God rested on its summit in the form of a cloud, but at night, the top was alight with fire. It was the reassurance of God's presence and protection.

After our camps were settled, I was called by God.

Moses, come to me on this mountain.

While hiking the steep slopes toward the cloud, I remembered many months ago while living in Midian that the I AM told me His people were to worship Him *on this mountain.* The first time I heard those words, I was terrified. But now entering the thickness of the cloud, I had to proceed cautiously and slowly because it was difficult to see. With confidence, I continued and waited for the voice of God.

Tell the people to prepare themselves today and tomorrow with fasting and prayer. Have them wash themselves and their clothes. On the third day, I will speak to them from the cloud on this mountain.

In my excitement, I hurried down the mountain. I gave the Israelites, God's chosen people, the instructions for preparing themselves to hear Him speak to them from this mountain.

On the morning of the third day, all eyes were looking at the mountain of God. The white cloud slowly turned dark and crept down the slopes until all of Mount Sinai was covered in an eerie darkness. From the darkness came flashes of lightning. Thunder echoed between the surrounding mountains. A tremendous trumpet blast became louder and louder, and the mountain shook to its very base. The top of the mountain was on fire, and the smoke of it rose as from a huge chimney.

God had spoken to me many times, but this demonstration of His mighty power and holiness was beyond my experience. I and all the people fell with our faces to the ground in extreme fear and trembling. The Great I AM was Omnipotent in the presence of our weakness! Omniscient in the presence of ignorance! Purity in the presence of contamination and filth.

Suddenly, the lightning and thundering ceased, and there were a few moments of complete silence. Silence and reverence! In the highest reverence, the voice of God was heard.

And God said,

> *You shall not have cherished desires for any person or object more than Me.*
>
> *You shall not make any images of heavenly deities to bow down to in worship, neither make any likenesses of the sky, land, or sea to worship.*
>
> *You shall not take the name of the Lord in vain. Anyone who uses the name of the Lord arrogantly by word or action is guilty of iniquity.*
>
> *Remember the Sabbath day to keep it holy for in six days, you, your family, and your servants shall do all your work, but the seventh day is the Sabbath for rest and worship of the Lord your God. The Lord created all things in six days and rested on the seventh day. Therefore, the seventh day is sacred and holy.*
>
> *Honor you father and your mother.*
>
> *You shall not murder.*
>
> *You shall not commit adultery.*
>
> *You shall not steal.*
>
> *You shall not bear false testimony.*
>
> *You shall not covet or crave anything that belongs to someone else.*

The people trembled with every word spoken by God, and in fear, they returned to their tents. A short time later, a delegation came to me saying, "Moses, *you* speak to us the words of God. We will hear you and obey, but let not God speak to us or we will die."

It was an awesome experience to see the power of God on Mount Sinai and to hear His voice, but I understood their fears. All of it seemed too overwhelming: the dark cloud, the lightning, the thunder, the earthquake, the fire, the smoke, the loud trumpet, and, finally, the powerful voice of the All Mighty. Yes, if God willed it, I would speak to the people *for* Him. I made many trips to the holy mountain of God and returned with instructions for His people.

CHAPTER 20

THE GOLDEN CALF/ COMMANDMENTS BROKEN

On one occasion, Joshua and I were both summoned by God to the mountain. Upon reaching the cloud, we waited for seven days for further instructions. We ate manna and drank from a stream provided by God while our faith and patience were tested. On the seventh day, which was the Sabbath, I was called to enter the cloud, and Joshua was told to wait for my return.

Make Me a Sanctuary that I may dwell among them.

For forty days, I received detailed instructions from God on how to build His Sanctuary—the structure itself, the objects, and the furniture within it. I was not prepared to write down all the meticulous details but was confident God would bring to my memory all that should be done for Him. This building project was to involve *all* the people of the camp—their gifts and their skills!

God cut two tablets of stone out of the mountain, and the Ten Commandments spoken by Him from the mountain were written on those stones by His own finger. Those two tablets were to be placed in the Ark of the Covenant in the Sanctuary.

With the precious stone tablets in my arms, I began my descent down the mountain.

Before meeting up with Joshua, God said, *Moses, your people, whom you brought from Egypt, have corrupted themselves. They have broken their promise to obey the covenant they made with Me. They have sinned greatly with idolatry, rebellion, and violence, and have made a calf of molten gold to worship, and have sacrificed to it. They are claiming this worthless hunk of gold brought them out of Egyptian slavery. They are a stiff-necked and obstinate people. Stand aside, Moses, and let me destroy them. Then I will make* you *a great nation.*

Please, Lord, it was not by my *power that brought these people out of Egypt. It was only by Your mighty hand and power that these people were set free from slavery. All the surrounding nations have now heard of the only true God—the Lord of the Universe. Why should Egypt say that You brought the Israelites here to destroy them? Remember Your promise that You would make them a great nation, with countless descendants as the stars of heaven. Please turn now from Your anger, and change Your mind about their destruction.*

After the forty days in the presence of God, I met with Joshua, and we began our descent from the mountain. Joshua noticed my melancholic demeanor but said nothing, assuming I was engulfed with the counsel from the I AM.

But I was fearful for the Israelites—God's children. Frightened for their future! Worried for their weakness! Trembling for their temptations! As we neared the base, we heard loud noises.

Joshua commented, "There is the sound of war coming from the camp. Has another warlike tribe attacked our people while we were on the mountain?"

With a heavy heart and sand in my throat, I replied, "No, Joshua. That is the sound of *sin* and *idolatry*."

While Joshua and I were on the holy mountain of Sinai, my brother, Aaron, was left in charge of the camp. The people waited for weeks for my return, and seeing occasional lightning coming from the cloud that covered the mountain, they feared my destruction, saying, "Look! There is lightning! Fire! Moses surely has been consumed by it. He has brought us here to die, but instead, *he* is dead! God has killed him!"

Restlessness and fear spread throughout the camp like a putrid infection—a ghastly disease, a loathsome plague. Some wanted to move on to Canaan by themselves, and some wanted to return to Egypt. Coming from a country with countless images of worthless deities, they wanted to see physical objects of their worship—not a cloud on top of a mountain!

Instigated mostly by the "mixed multitude"—the Egyptians who joined us in the exodus—a demand rang out that an image be made to one of their heathen gods that they may pay homage and sacrifice to it. Some of the conscientious and faithful few strongly objected and resisted such sinful idolatry.

But Aaron, being weak and fearful for his own life, acquiesced to their demands.

"Bring me your gold earrings and bracelets that I may make a molten calf for you, like the ones in Egypt. A god that you can see, a god that you can worship, a god that you can offer sacrifices to."

Hathor, the goddess of love and protection, was sometimes portrayed as a female with the head of a cow and sometimes just as a cow itself. There were other deities, like Apis the Bull, that were among the bovine Egyptian gods. When the molten calf was formed, it was placed on top of a grouping of large stones that displayed multiple paintings and etchings of cows and bulls. When all was finished, the people danced and shouted, "*These* are your gods, oh Israel, which brought you out of Egypt."

When Aaron saw how pleased they were with the golden calf, he built an altar in front of it, saying, "Tomorrow will be a feast to the Lord."

A feast? Yes! To the "Lord?" *No!* The feasting included gluttony and licentiousness! Dancing and Drunkenness! Laughing and Lewdness! Vulgarity and violence! Certainly not a feast to the Lord, our God!

When Joshua and I approached the camp, we saw the wickedness and dancing around the golden calf at the base of God's holy mountain. Even though I had been told of this sin and God's inclination to destroy these people, I was still shocked to my deepest core at what I saw. My knees buckled, and my stomach irrupted. My anger burned inside me like a volcano, and I regretted my pleading for their lives. Perhaps God had every right to desire to wipe them off the face of the earth.

In the darkness of the evening hour, I saw the flames leaping from the altar in front of the golden calf, an idol and an abomination. Other torches of fire were being waved around as people were dancing about in lewd revelry, reminding me of scenes of Egypt. Egypt, the land of thousands of worthless gods! There seemed to be an ominous darkness, not attributed to the hour but a heaviness of evil that surrounded the drunken rabble. My eyes burned, and my heart was crushed as I yelled, "No! No!" But my protest was as useless as howling under water or whispering into the wind.

Consumed with anger, I lifted the stones of God's Ten Commandments above my head and, with all my strength, threw them at the reveling mob. The word of God was shattered at the foot of the mountain. Both physically and in principle, every one of God's commandments was broken! The singing, the shouting, and the laughter hushed. The dancing ceased. The tambourines, lutes, trumpets, and drums were mute. All eyes were on me.

In strength beyond my human ability, I tore down the golden idol. I ground it into powder, threw it into the water, and made the people drink it. Now, they could see that their god was defenseless to resist its destruction—truly a worthless god!

Then turning to Aaron, I asked incredulously, "How on earth did this happen? How could these people do such a thing while you were in charge? You were the leader appointed by *God* in my absence! Why did you not stop them from doing such a vile and sinful thing?"

"Don't be angry with me, Moses. You know these people and their wickedness. They were afraid you were not returning from the mountain and that you were probably dead. You were gone so long! They wanted a god that would lead them, a god they could see and touch. Some of the people who resisted the idea of an idol were killed by those who demanded it. I was afraid too, Moses! All I did was to ask them to bring me their gold earrings. When I threw the gold into the fire, out came the golden calf."

Out came the golden calf? Really? A miracle? No! No! Absolutely not! Never! Incomprehensible! Impossible!

The blame for this great sin was hurled like arrows at many people, including *me* for "abandoning" them. The idolatrous rebels blamed me and ultimately God for leaving them "leaderless." No one stood alone to take the blame or admit their guilt. The strongest instigators of this rebellion were led by the "mixed multitude." They feared being left alone in the wilderness without a god they could *see* and worship. In recognizing Aaron's weakness of leadership, they became bolder and more threatening in their demands.

Was Aaron to blame? For those who have been given much evidence of God's goodness and power, much more was required of them! Aaron had personally witnessed the many wonders and the omnipotent authority of God in Egypt, at the Red Sea, and on Mount Sinai. In addition, he had been given the authority by God to rule in my absence. It was Aaron's responsibility to be strong in the Lord however painful or dangerous that might have been to him.

Yes, I too have been threatened by stoning, and I understand his fear. And yet…

With sincere brokenness and cleansing tears cascading down his aged cheeks, Aaron repented of his weakness and his contribution to this grievous sin. Now, I too, with heavy weeping, pleaded with God to save his life as I had previously pleaded for the lives of His people.

The camp was now divided into three groups: those who had resisted the idolatry and were innocent of its corruption, those who partook in the sinful activity but were truly repentant of their involvement; and finally, those who continued to be angry, treasonous, and stubbornly resistant in their rebellion. When all was said and done, the ringleaders and three thousand unrepentant men and women were destroyed. Sad! Tragic! However, this was necessary to show God's people and the surrounding nations that idolatry was not tolerated by the true and living God of heaven. The seeds of rebellion had to be eradicated, or the seeds would take root and grow again.

Still, a cry arose that the camp of Israel should now leave the wilderness and "take" Canaan as promised by God. But this was not in the will of the Lord at this time.

FROM HAUGHTY TO HUMBLE

Tabernacle Furniture

Chapter 21

The Tabernacle/ Commandments Written

After the Ten Commandments of stone written by the finger of God were shattered both physically and morally, I carved out another two large tablets of stone and returned to the holy mountain. I was on Sinai, the mountain of God, for another forty days, communicating and witnessing, face-to-face, the goodness of God. Upon my return from the mountain, and unbeknownst to me, my face shone like the sun, and the people were afraid to approach me. I then veiled my face whenever I returned from the presence of God until the brightness eventually faded.

After a period of genuine repentance, and sensing their longing for the evidence of God's acceptance, I gave the people God's instructions for a Sanctuary to be built that He may dwell with them. An invitation went throughout the camp to bring their gold and riches obtained as payment for their many years of slavery in Egypt. They responded with much enthusiasm! With such an overwhelming presentation of offerings and sacrifice, I was prompted to have them suspend and hold back their giving.

"People, God is very pleased with your freewill gifts for His Sanctuary. Stop! Bring no more because we have enough, enough materials for God's dwelling house among us.

"People, now we need skilled men and women to put this temple together as God has instructed. Come and present your talents, and we will choose from among you for this honor."

Again, their willingness was almost overwhelming. Many men who had worked in and around the palace of the Pharaoh as skilled workmen with gold, silver, bronze, and wood were chosen to build the temple and make the furniture. Women with great talent for sewing, weaving, and embroidery made drapery, curtains, veils, and robes to be worn by the priests, who were Aaron and his sons. Those who were not directly involved with the building or the ornamenting of the temple helped in many other ways. They took on the responsibility of helping with cooking, cleaning, childcare, and caring for the herds. There was a genuine eagerness throughout the camp to be involved with this tribute to God and His dwelling place among us.

After about six months, the tabernacle was finished. Its beautiful gold furniture and the elaborately embroidered silver angels on the curtain separating the Holy Place from the Most Holy Place reflected the light from the seven golden candlesticks. Two other pieces of furniture adorned the Holy Place—the Altar of Incense and the Table of Shewbread.

The ark was a gold-covered wooden chest with a lid of pure gold. At the ends of the chest were two cherubim of pure gold whose wings spread up and over the chest. The cherubim faced each other and looked downward toward the top of the lid, which was called the Mercy Seat. The tablets of stone on which the Lord Himself had engraved the Ten Commandments with His own finger (for the second time) were reverently placed inside this special chest of gold—the ark of the covenant. It was the only piece of furniture in the Most Holy Place.

When the Tabernacle was finished, the Israelites congregated around it in reverence and satisfaction at its appearance and purpose. In silence and awe, the people witnessed the acceptance and blessing from the King of kings, the Lord of lords, the Lord omnipotent forever and ever. In the witness of all the Israelites, a pillar of cloud hovered briefly over the sanctuary before it completely enveloped and filled the blessed structure. And for a period of time, no one was able to enter the sanctuary. Eventually, the glorious presence of God settled over the Ark of the Covenant. This presence was called the Shechinah.

I am thrilled and humbled to be part of this blessing from the Great IAM. Surely, the children of Israel will now rededicate themselves to keeping forever the covenant of our God.

The Ten Commandments
[In Early Semitic (Sinaiatic) Hebrew]

FROM HAUGHTY TO HUMBLE

Chapter 22

Miriam's Rebellion

Aaron and Miriam were greatly blessed by God, who gave them wisdom and the gift of prophecy. Miriam was especially skilled in music and poetry. Aaron was chosen to be the high priest of the tabernacle. They helped me greatly in lessening my burden of leadership. Both held elevated positions of influence and were highly regarded as chosen by God.

Different events, however, caused both Miriam and Aaron to question why I had listened to advice from Jethro, my father-in-law, regarding the appointment of judges. And in other matters, they felt I had overlooked or not sought *their* counsel. Insidious at first, they felt God had given them equal leadership as was given to me. Their *covert* mumbling turned to unbridled envy until they eventually faced me with *open* rebellion. Dark clouds of discontent hovered with their questioning.

"Are you the only one, Moses, to whom God has spoken? Hasn't he also revealed His will to us? Do we not prophecy in His name? Are we not equally favored by God?"

Sadly, Miriam did not approve of my marriage to Zipporah because she was not Hebrew but was a Cushite woman and of very dark skin. But my wife worshipped the true God and was *also* a descendant of Abraham. The moment these two women met, I noticed aloofness in Miriam's dark eyes. She implied displeasure toward the nationality of my shy wife and presented herself as a *preferred* Israelite. Miriam resented what she perceived as Zipporah's influence on me. At first, the situation was subtle and went unnoticed by my wife's naivety. But this festering undercurrent of resentment eventually turned to ill-disguised contempt. There was palpable tension between my timid wife and my strong-willed, assertive sister.

Miriam blamed Zipporah for preventing me from seeking counsel from her and Aaron. Not recognizing the first seeds of jealousy, Aaron was eventually persuaded to sympathize with Miriam and share her resentment and bitterness. Aaron's weakness and gentle spirit were no match for Miriam's intense resolutions. In open hostility, my brother and sister came to me with their grievances. They demonstrated mutiny against me and the Great I AM!

Facing me in front of the tabernacle, Aaron and Miriam were confronted by God.

In the pillar cloud above the sanctuary, a Voice said to them, *I have spoken to you and other prophets through visions and dreams. But not so with my servant, Moses, who is faithful to Me. With*

Moses, I speak face-to-face openly, and he sees My form. Why then were you not afraid to speak against My servant, Moses?

At that point, the cloud disappeared, and Miriam instantly became leprous. Her skin turned white as death and destined *for* death. Falling to their knees, Miriam and Aaron confessed their sin of rebellion, for their contribution to the spreading of acrimony, for their pride, for their bitterness and jealousy toward me, and especially for sinning against the Great I AM.

Both Aaron and I pled with God for the life of our beloved sister, Miriam. God removed His presence from the tabernacle until Miriam was taken outside the camp, where she was certain to die of leprosy, unless, through our prayers, she was granted healing by God.

Miriam remained banished outside the camp for seven days until she was healed of this most dreaded and deadly disease. The whole camp rejoiced at her return. She was clean! Miriam's singing was again heard in praises to our God.

Oh, God, hear us in our weakness. Give us the strength to follow Your will and to hold on tightly to Your commandments. Protect us from straying away from Your will. Lead us in the paths of righteousness. Thank You for Your gracious love and forgiveness.

Miriam

Chapter 23

THE TWELVE SPIES AT CANAAN

There were many ups and downs while traveling through this wilderness. Murmurings and mutinies, praises and prayers, threats and trauma, faith and forgiveness.

There was excitement throughout the Israelite nation as we traveled north and close to the borders of the promised land. Children were running and playing tag. The women were singing as they played their lutes and tambourines. Even our herds seemed to anticipate greener pastures. It appeared that everyone was in one accord with anticipation, seeing the fulfillment of the promise made to Israel over four hundred years ago.

We set up camp to rest before preparing for our inheritance of Canaan, the promised land, the land of milk and honey. It was suggested by a small delegation that we first send spies to check out the cities of the land and to see how strong and fortified their walls were.

"We should know what the people are like before we enter. Are their markets full? Are their pastures, orchards, and vineyards productive?"

Oh, Israel, doesn't it mean anything to you that God said He will give us the land of milk and honey? "Give" means a gift. "Milk and honey" mean productive and sweet. Where is your faith? Where is your trust that God will do what He says He will do for you?

After going to the Lord with the people's request for spies, I was given permission to choose twelve honorable men, one from each tribe, to serve as secret agents. They were to survey the land before us. After the spies left, we settled back to await their return and report.

After forty days, the twelve spies returned with exciting information about the fruitfulness of the land. They brought back a variety of fruits and huge clusters of grapes carried on poles by some of the men.

"This is truly the land of milk and honey, and this is a sampling of their harvests."

After their description of the beauty and abundance of lush lands, there descended an ominous dark cloud of fear that emanated from ten of the spies. With frowns, shaking heads, and exaggerated fighting stances, those spies shouted that taking Canaan would not be possible.

"Infeasible! Futile! Their cities have high walls that are well fortified. The men are giants, and we are mere grasshoppers in comparison to them. It will be impossible to conquer them."

Had these men forgotten how grasshoppers morphed into overpowering locust and ate everything that was green in Egypt? With God's help, we can take this land!

Anger and fear spread like wildfire on dry tinder. Their hope of the promised land was overshadowed by despair and panic. Their faith in God, who had delivered them from Egypt and given them all their needs, was forgotten!

Finally, one of the twelve spies, Caleb, shouted, above the crying, "People of God, heirs of Abraham, Isaac, and Jacob. You have been *promised* this land. Yes, the city's walls are high, and the Canaanites are strong, but God has promised to *give* this land to us. Let us go and receive our inheritance. Through God's leading, we are well able to overcome it."

After hearing Caleb and Joshua's report and encouragement, a brief hush engulfed the people who were previously fearful of going into Canaan. But the other ten spies again incited everyone to join in their opposition against Caleb, Joshua, me, and ultimately God. They had distorted the truth to gain their control. Lies, exaggerations, and intimidations! Open revolt and mutiny quickly followed and spread over the people like a contagious plague.

After a night of wailing, they came to me threateningly.

"What does God want for us? To die in Egypt or die in the wilderness? We will choose a better leader than you, Moses. We will elect a captain who will lead and return us to Egypt."

Return to Egypt where they were mere slaves and where they had suffered so much? Had any of them suffered after leaving Egypt?

The voices of Joshua and Caleb were heard above the uncontrolled behaviors and cries of the mob.

"Don't rebel against God. We are able to inherit Canaan. God will take away their defenses and give us victory! *Victory!*"

Suddenly, another cry arose, instigated by the ten rebel spies, to kill Joshua and Caleb, who were standing in front of the tabernacle. With stones in their hands and hate in their hearts, they brazenly approached the men who encouraged the Israelites to trust in the God of their salvation. Instantly, the cloud over the tabernacle flashed a brilliant radiance. The brightness caused the ten mutinous spies to drop their stones and run to their tents.

God said to me, *I will destroy these rebellious people with a pestilence. I will disinherit them and make you, Moses, a great nation.*

For the second time, I pleaded with God not to terminate His people and bring shame to His name.

Lord, the surrounding nations would glory in their destruction and deny the miraculous events surrounding the Israelites' exodus from Egypt. Have mercy on Your children, and give me wisdom.

An additional message came from God to the Israelites.

As you have spoken to My servant, Moses, I will speak to you. To those of you who are twenty years and older, your dead bodies shall fall in the wilderness. After forty years, I will bring your young ones to the promised land, the land which you have despised. As for Caleb and Joshua, they will enter into the land at the appointed time. Return now to the wilderness by the Red Sea.

In the sight of all Israel, the ten defiant spies died of a plague. Seeing the hand of God, the people *claimed* to be sorry for their rebellion, not sorry for disbelieving but sorry for God's judgment!

In their boldness, they said, "We will *not* return to the wilderness, according to God's command! We will arm ourselves with weapons of war and take Canaan by force and by our own power."

Oh, Israel, it was never in God's plan to fight for the promised land but to inherit it as a gift. And now, oh, foolish Israelites, God has forbidden you to go into Canaan but to return to the wilderness.

The Canaanites had heard of the mysterious wonders that protected this large nation close to their borders. For fear of disaster, they *dared* not be the aggressors, but they summoned the strong Amalekites to help protect their lands. Then they positioned and secured themselves on a flat rocky summit overlooking the Israelite encampment.

When I saw the large multitude of our men with armor, spears, and swords planning to climb the embankment toward the well-fortified Army, I ran to them, pleading, "Please do not attempt this foolishness. God has forbidden this. You shall not prosper! This folly is doomed for failure!"

In their arrogance, and without the Ark or the blessings of God, the self-appointed Army was leaderless as they approached the steep slopes. They determined to gain by force the land that God had now forbidden them to have for forty years.

The attack was a dismal failure as huge rocks came thundering down causing defeat, injury, and death to the rebel Army. Forced to retreat, the survivors of the insurgent troops wept before God, who turned a deaf ear to their cries.

With the defeat of the Israelite nation, the Canaanites boasted, "We have heard many stories about the protection given to the Israelites by their God. With this easy defeat and no harm done to us, we now believe those reports to be false. Take heart men of Canaan, there is no cause to fear these impudent Israelites."

CHAPTER 24

KORAH'S REBELLION/ DEATH OF MIRIAM

With heavy hearts, we packed our camp and the tabernacle and headed south into the wilderness by the Red Sea. This was a great disappointment to everyone—no singing and no rejoicing. For months, they had complained about petty inconveniences, but now God had given them something about which they could really cry.

With tremendous sadness, the Israelite nation slowly returned to the wilderness, saying, "The blessing of entering the promised land has been removed from us by God due to our rebellion, mutiny, and self-pride. Now, we will die, and our bodies will cover the wastelands. We will be food for vultures and scavengers. Our bones will bleach in the desert sun. Only our children will inherit the promise given to our father, Israel."

Oh, God, had I failed in leadership? Could I have been stronger or a better representative of your command? Please give me patience and wisdom to lead Your people for forty years!"

For a while, all seemed in harmony with repentance and cooperation until rebellion imperceptibly began to rear its ugly and dangerous head again.

Korah, a cousin of mine and of the tribe of Levi, was a member of the tabernacle service. Cautiously, he began to whisper his dissatisfaction of not being given the honor of *priesthood*. Because of his influence among the people, he gained a secret following of sympathizers for his perceived *indignity*.

"Moses is responsible for our returning to this wilderness. It is *his* fault if we die here! His desire for our wealth and possessions is behind our failure to take ownership of Canaan. Has God spoken *only* to Moses? No! God has spoken to *me* and has empowered *me* to take leadership of the tabernacle *and* the government. Listen to *me, you Israelites*! We are God's *holy* people, a *righteous* people, not 'sinners' as Moses has pronounced on us."

Korah's desire for higher honors and power had gradually turned his appalling jealousy into treacherous rebellion toward Aaron and me. He and his confidants stealthily acquired 250 influential supporters for his cause. They were led to believe in Korah's crusade—to make the Israelite nation stronger and happier. His continual praises and words of approval toward the people inspired them to look to Korah as their new leader.

With one accord, they shouted, "For God and His *holy* people!"

Korah's intent was to make himself higher than the temple servants that were *appointed by God*, superior than the *word* of God.

A similar episode of pride and ambition happened in Heaven when Lucifer became envious and jealous of the Son of God. He desired to make himself higher than the stars of heaven and worthy of worship. Lucifer's grievance against God, and his flattery toward the other angels, caused many of them to believe and side with him, a conviction that resulted in their banishment from heaven.

An undercurrent of rebellion now grew until sufficient support gave Korah the courage, along with his entourage of two close associates and 250 men aspiring to be priests, to approach Aaron and me with open mutiny in front of the tabernacle.

"Moses, you make *yourself* higher and holier than the people. It is *your* fault that we were taken from Egypt. It is *your* fault that our Army failed taking Canaan. It is *your* fault we are not in the promised land. It is *your* fault we are back in the wilderness. All the people are now demanding an enlightened and progressive leader. Only I can fulfill that position, and I now have the support of *all* Israel!"

Unsuspecting of this rebellion and these false accusations, my heart was pierced to the point of breaking, and I fell to my knees. Many times, I had been accused of leading the Israelites into the desert to die of thirst or hunger for my own gain but not by such a large mob of hostiles. These were leading men of Israel who were also considered to be my friends.

Oh, God, give me the wisdom to deal with these rebels. If I have displeased You, I stand alone and accept Your judgment. Only You can judge me. Only You are in control. Please give me Your words and Your wisdom.

With calmness and divine guidance, I stood before them and announced, "Tomorrow, God will choose who will be His priests. Those who aspire to be priests are to bring censers with incense to the tabernacle."

The next day, and in their arrogance, the 250 men, carrying their censers of burning incense, walked boldly inside the tabernacle courtyard. In defiance, Korah, Dathan, and Abriam returned to their tents.

It amazes me that the Israelites, who have witnessed the blessings and the judgments of God, feel free to continually challenge the Great I AM. Jealousy and conspiracy brought leprosy to Miriam. Nadab and Abihu were struck by God for burning unauthorized fire in their censers. Don't these men, Korah and his rebels fear God? Do they think they are in control and can do anything they wish? What gives them the audacity to confront the authority of God?

In the judgment of the Great I AM, the earth opened up and swallowed the three chief conspirators, Korah, Dathan, and Abriam, with their families and all their possessions. Then fire flashed from the cloud above the tabernacle and consumed the 250 men with their censers.

In terror, but not in repentance, the people ran, scattering like cockroaches in the light for fear they might also be swallowed by the earth. Without remorse, they knew they shared in the guilt of this rebellion. Though the power and authority of God were evidences enough of His judgment, their sympathies went out to those who were slain.

Through the flattery of Korah, they refused to believe they were anything but holy and that I, Moses, had raised myself over them for my own pleasure and self-esteem. All their sorrows and the decree to wander forty years in the wilderness were put on *my* shoulders. I was blamed for taking them out of Egypt to suffer and die in the desert. I was responsible for their defeat at the borders of Canaan. It was my fault for their forty years in the wilderness. I had deceived and abused them for my own glory. And now they accused me of *killing* "the people of the Lord and good men"—men who would free them from condemnation of sin and men who would lead them to conquer Canaan or return them to Egypt.

Murmuring, rebellion, and accusations against Aaron and me continued until fourteen thousand Israelites died of a plague. Still, questions arose whether the privilege of priesthood was given *only* to the family of Aaron. By the divine direction of God, all the tribes were to engrave the name of their tribe on a rod and present it to the Tabernacle. These rods from each of the twelve tribes were laid before the Ark of the Covenant.

The next morning, the rod with Aaron's name and tribe had blossomed and yielded almonds. The miracle of Aaron's rod was shown to the people, who agreed that his divine appointment was indeed ordained by God.

*****

Miriam, our beloved sister, died while we were camped in Kadesh. Wonderful memories flooded my mind of her watching over me and my basket floating on the crocodile-infested Nile River. How brave she was to approach the Egyptian princess to suggest a nurse for my care! She led the singing after our miraculous crossing of the Red Sea! Miriam was greatly blessed with talents of music and poetry. She was healed of leprosy. She was sanctified as a prophet of God and was highly respected among the people.

Aaron and I had noticed that our older sister had begun to slow down considerably. With her death approaching, we tenderly watched over her and protected her from the elements of heat or cold.

In Miriam's sweet voice, she whispered, "Please, brothers, my time is near. You must be strong for God and for His people. Take heart I will see you in heaven."

The entire Israelite encampment mourned the passing of this sweet old lady, Miriam.

Chapter 25

The Sin of Moses

The period of wandering forty years in the wilderness was nearly over. There had been good times and bad times! Praises and rebellions! Still, whenever there was an inconvenience or a perceived problem, the people were quick to complain and blame Aaron and me.

Dear God in heaven, lead us now into the promised land, the land promised to our father, Israel. Guide our steps, fill our hearts, and give us faith to follow You.

We traveled north again and camped a little distance from Edom, which belonged to the descendants of Esau. Our food and water supply were no longer supplied by God, who said, *You will pass through the city belonging to your brothers, the children of Esau. They will be afraid of you and let you pass through their city unmolested. It is a fruitful land, and you will buy from them water to drink and food to eat.*

Fear and doubt again filled the Israelites. They had always been *freely* supplied with enough water for themselves and their animals. The thought of traveling through the land belonging to Esau's descendants and *buying* the food and water they needed was rejected. It was refused. They began to feel that there was no hope of ever seeing the land promised to them.

"Moses, why did you bring us into this wilderness to die along with our cattle? There is no water here! You expect us to *buy* our food and water? We should have died with our fathers."

Lord, I am so tired of this complaining. Doesn't it occur to these people that You are leading them through Edom, the best route to Canaan? For forty years, I have been blamed for taking them out of Egypt… Egypt! Most of these people don't even remember Egypt! You have supplied all their needs, and yet they complain. And now, they are demanding water! Lord, my patience is gone!

Moses, I want you and Aaron to gather the people and take them to the rock, which I will show you. Stand before the rock and speak to it. Then water will come out of the rock for the people.

Aaron and I stood before the appointed rock and looked out at the mutinous mob.

Anger and impatience filled our hearts, and I yelled, "Hear me, you defiant rebels. Must *we* make water spew out of this rock for you?"

After I spoke those profane words, I struck the rock twice with my rod! At once, I knew I had sinned. I had disobeyed the command of God to "speak to the rock." I had lost my temper and expressed uncontrolled anger. Yet God still caused water to gush out of the rock in great abundance as He had done *forty* years ago that split the rock in the desert.

Immediately, God spoke to Aaron and me, *Because you have not believed Me nor obeyed My command in full view of the children of Israel, you shall not bring them into the promised land."* Amen—and Amen!

With sincere regret and repentance, my brother and I accepted our sentence of being denied entrance into the land promised to Israel. We would die as did the rebellious Israelites during the last forty years. Our bones would also be bleached in the desert sun. Though their sins had been great, Aaron and I were held to a higher standard as representatives of God and of His commands. God accepted our heartfelt remorse with forgiveness, but our sudden and sinful anger could not be overlooked—for the sake of the people.

I announced, "Children of Israel, I have pleaded with God to amend His sentence and allow Aaron and me to enter into the promised land with you, but my appeal has been denied."

As hurtful and disappointing as God's decision was, the people needed to see the consequence of sin. The strongest temptation could not excuse sin! In all their murmurings against me for forty years, the people could now see that the Great I AM was their *true leader*—not me!

*****

God had promised the Israelites safe passage to the promised land through Edom. Close to its borders, polite messages were sent twice to the king of Edom, asking for safe passage through his lands. Twice, a threatening refusal was returned to the Israelites with the promise of war should we attempt to cross over their borderline.

Instead of believing and trusting in the promise of God of "safe passage" *through* Edom, fear and murmuring prevailed. Again, the Israelites' unbelief became their punishment! Again, we had to return south to the desert wastelands! The wastelands seemed harsher and more dangerous now, especially after seeing the green hills and valleys of Edom.

Oh, God, when will Your people learn to trust You? Haven't You supplied all their needs—their food, their water? There are none who are crippled or feeble. Their clothes and their shoes have not worn out. So far, they have been protected from the hazards of the desert, shielded from scorpions, biting insects, poisonous snakes. Must they now learn these dangers?

Chapter 26

The Death of Aaron

We traveled south again and came close to Mount Hor when God spoke to me, *Take Aaron and his son, Eleazar, to the summit of this mountain. Then take all of Aaron's priestly garments from him and put them on Eleazar. There, Aaron will die.*

Due to our disobedience, I knew Aaron's death was approaching, but it was still heartbreaking to lose my brother—my best friend. For many years, he was a great comfort to me, and we stood side by side in the service of God. We stood together in front of Pharaoh. We crossed the Red Sea together and saw the destruction of Pharaoh's Army. Many times, we suffered because of the abuse and threats from rebellious mobs. We worked hard to prepare the Israelites for their promised inheritance. And finally, we looked forward to entering the promised land *with* God's people.

Our steep assent to the top of Mount Hor was slow and difficult. Aaron and I were both very old men with white hair and white beards. We rested often, not wanting to end our close relationship. We shared laughter and tears and talked about our wilderness wanderings. But mostly, we prayed for the future of God's people in Canaan.

Slowly and with care, removing Aaron's priestly breastplate and robes was a devastating task for me and for his son. Our tears made it exceedingly difficult to transfer these holy garments onto Eleazar—God's appointed High Priest. While transferring Eleazar's clothes onto himself, Aaron had *no* tears coming from his aged eyes. This righteous servant of God had a smile and a peaceful expression on his face. Only praises came from his lips as we hugged and clung to each other. After fulfilling God's instructions, we sat down and leaned against a large rock—*a rock!* Instantly, both of us remembered the *Rock* that gave lifesaving water, and we were comforted resting against this *Rock*.

After the strain of the mountain climb, the transfer of the holy vestments, and the stress of the anticipated event, we closed our eyes and waited. Leaning in my arms, Aaron was serene. He was assured of God's forgiveness and began humming a song our sister, Miriam, had written. He was confident of eternal life in heaven with the Great I AM. A short time later, my beloved brother took his last breath. There on Mount Hor, and with the help of an angel of God, we buried Aaron.

Oh, God, how I miss my brother, my constant companion! How I miss his gentle spirit. How I miss his words of comfort and encouragement! Please forgive me if I now long to join my brother in death. I am old, I am tired, I am ready, Lord.

Aaron

CHAPTER 27

VENOMOUS SNAKES/ BALAAM'S CURSE

After a period of mourning for the death of Aaron, we continued our long trek southward to the dry, hot, and desolate desert. Tired and thirsty, the people complained and complained! Instead of admitting their sin of not trusting in God, they again blamed me for their returning to the wilderness. How soon they forgot their sins, their doubt, and their rebellion. They continually talked about their problems and their desire to return to Egypt. Their constant grumbling was driving them further away from their belief in the One, who had protected them from the harshness of wilderness living. It now felt as if we were traveling alone and moving into a hostile and dangerous land.

Moses, because of the rebellion of these people and their refusal to acknowledge My divine protection from the countless dangers, which were a constant threat, I will withdraw from them. Their past murmurings will soon seem petty in their own eyes. I will permit death by the poisonous snakes that are numerous in this wilderness. They will come to understand real *trouble, which will be a certainty, until they humble themselves and repent.*

A horde of aggressive and venomous snakes invaded the whole camp, reminding me of the destructive plagues of Egypt. Nearly every family was affected with poisonous bites causing pain and death. No one was safe. No more were the Israelites complaining of the manna and wishing for *different* bread. No more were there wishes to return to Egypt. No more were they bickering and fighting among themselves.

With humbleness, they said, "Moses, we have sinned against God and you. Please pray to God on our behalf and ask that He forgive our sins. Ask also that He remove these serpents before we *all* die."

In response to my prayer on behalf of the people, God told me, *Make a serpent of brass, and twist it around a poll. Elevate it so that everyone may see it. Those who have been bitten, and are alive, are commanded to look at it that they may live.*

Some looked at the brass serpent and lived, but others said, "That is foolishness! How can simply *looking* at a metal snake save my life?"

Some, even those who were dying and carried on cots, looked at the serpent in faith and lived. Many others perished. This was such a *simple* test of faith. Just look and live! And yet...

*****

Over the next few months, we traveled north again. Through the guidance of the Pillar, and the power of God, we conquered the giant kings of Gilead and Bashan. We briefly occupied their lands until we moved north of the Dead Sea, beside the Jordan River, and east of Canaan. We camped there in preparation for entry into the promised land.

Because of our victory over Gilead and Bashan, the king of Moab greatly feared us. Due to this fear, he was unwilling to attempt any direct attack on the Israelite nation.

Realizing he had no power of his own, Balak, the king of Moab, sought a sorcerer and a prophet of God to "curse" our nation. Balaam, the prophet, was promised riches and honor to pronounce anathema on the Israelites. He had full knowledge of Israel's God, but his heart was ambivalent. With the promise of riches and honor, Balaam, who was morally weak and honor seeking, made three attempts to curse Israel but to no avail. The God of Israel would not allow it.

Balak blurted, "I asked you to *curse* these people not bless them! Because you have not done as I requested, neither will I honor you with riches."

Bowing low before the king, Balaam said, "Oh, King Balak, if you will seduce these Israelites into the worship of *your* gods, Baal and Ashtoreth, and beguile them with music, dancing, and seductive women, they will abandon *their* God and destroy *themselves*."

Realizing this plan had excellent potential, King Balak agreed and enlisted the help of Balaam to carry out the plan.

Soon, great apostasy filled the camp with bold and open idol worship, along with abhorrent lascivious relationships. As a result of their brazen disregard of God's commandments, a terrible plague followed, causing the deaths of tens of thousands. Thus, the last of the generations cursed to die in the wilderness, and not enter the promised land, was fulfilled. Now, Caleb and Joshua will be the only ones of that older age group to enter Canaan!

Many felt the punishment of Israel was just and, with deep sorrow and humiliation, confessed their sins in front of the Tabernacle.

God said to me, *The judgments are not for Israel alone. Choose one thousand men from all the tribes to avenge my people that the idolatrous nations and their kings will feel My judgments upon them. After that, you will be gathered with your ancestors.*

CHAPTER 28

THE DEATH OF MOSES

Standing on the shore of the Jordan River, looking across to the lush land of Canaan, all was ready, and it was fully evident that our possession of the promised land was at hand. I was reminded by God that I was not to enter the land with His children.

Oh, Lord God, only through Your power have Your people come this far as was promised to our father, Israel. Through your mercy, I have been forgiven of my weaknesses. I pray now that you will let me go into that good land beyond the Jordan.

Moses, don't ask Me again for My answer remains the same.

Oh, God, even as a child at my mother's knee, 120 years ago, I was encouraged and looked forward to seeing the promised land, the beautiful land You promised to our ancestor, Israel! Being denied entry along with the people I love is harder than all the trials I have endured for the past forty years. Yet, Lord, I will accept and respect Your verdict. Oh, God, now that we are at the borders of the promised land, who will lead them after I am gone? Who will speak Your words to them?

My faithful servant, Joshua, is filled with the Holy Spirit. Take him before Eleazar, the priest, and all the people. Put your hands on him in blessings. Your leadership responsibilities will be transferred from you and entrusted upon him. After that, you will go up alone to Mount Nebo and up to the pinnacle of Pisgah. I will show you the vast land to be given to My people. Then I will show you the future events for all mankind, even to the end of the age, and the Kingdom of Heaven.

God then gave me further instructions.

Before turning over your responsibilities to My servant, Joshua, call all the people together to review with them their history from Egypt until now. Remind them especially of the crossing of the Red Sea, the destruction of Pharaoh's Army, the Ten Commandments written by My finger, the building of the Tabernacle, the assurance and provision of food and water in the dry desert. If My people will follow all of My Commandments, I will be their God, and I will protect them! Don't be concerned about what to say. I will put the words in your mouth as I did in Egypt and have done throughout these forty trying years.

In reviewing and telling these Israelites their history, I realized that many of them had been too young to remember Egypt or the crossing of the Red Sea. They didn't remember receiving the Ten Commandments directly from God. Still, others were born *in* the wilderness and knew of nothing else. It was vitally important that they knew from where they came and why they were going into the promised land.

It never ceased to amaze me that when I spoke the words of God to His people, every eye could see me, and every word was heard. Thousands upon thousands could receive God's words through one man.

With Joshua beside me, I directed the people's attention to the task at hand and God's most recent instructions, the transfer of my leadership onto Joshua.

As instructed, I took Joshua, the son of Nun, before Eleazar, the priest. In solemnness, I laid my hands on God's chosen leader of His people and announced to the congregation the honor placed on Joshua that they will be obedient. In humbleness of spirit, many tears were shed by the people.

*****

There seemed to be much more I wanted to say, especially to those close to me, but my throat was tight and dry. How do I say "goodbye" to those I love, knowing I would never see them again this side of Heaven? How do I turn and walk away, rejecting their desire to be with me? How do I dry *their* tears? How do I dry *my* tears? How do I explain that I must do this *alone*?

My sons and my precious wife had long since died. Miriam and Aaron were also dead. I am alone!

You will go up alone *to Mount Nebo.* Alone—*alone!*

Slowly, I walked toward Mount Nebo with only my staff in my hand, the staff I used caring for Jethro's sheep, the staff that turned into a viper at the burning bush, the staff I held while standing in front of Pharaoh, the staff I raised at the parting and the closing of the Red Sea, the staff I used for forty years in the wilderness, the staff I used to strike the Rock—twice! The *staff* was not at fault—the fault was *mine*! My frustration, my anger, and my failure!

I progressed slowly up the mountain. The slow pace was not due to my old age. Since my hair and beard were white, I *looked* old, but I was still a stalwart man—sturdy hands, straight back, sonorous voice, and strong eyesight!

I felt strong enough to continue to into the… *Forgive me, Lord. I must not dwell on what is not mine to have. I must remember and be thankful for the things I have been given.*

Upon reaching the top of Mount Nebo, I took a deep breath and looked around. Suddenly, a panorama of green valleys, rich fields, ripe vineyards, and fruit-laden trees opened up before my eyes. In all directions, I saw abundance that was not common in the wilderness of Arabia beside the Red Sea. The sight was thrilling!

After that, I was shown the future of my people and *all* the people of the world. I saw many kings, good and evil. I saw a beautiful temple of God being built, destroyed, rebuilt, and then destroyed again. I saw the Sabbath being defiled. I saw it being defended. I saw the birth, the life, and the death of the promised Messiah. I saw violence and confusion. I saw the closing of this world's history. I saw the coming of the Messiah, surrounded by millions of angels. I saw people rejoicing at the sight of God's return, along with an untold number of people being raised from the dead to meet their Savior in the sky. I saw the Heavenly Sanctuary and the awesome City of God.

This overview was, for the most part, extremely disturbing as I could see rebellion, wickedness, wars, earthquakes, pestilence, plagues, and famines. It was such a sad and devastating panorama that thankfully ended with the most glorious reward given to those who were faithful to the Great I AM.

I was exhausted and thirsty, and I fell to my knees. Memories of my past flooded my mind—my beautiful wife, my talented sister, and my faithful brother. I had been face-to-face with powerful Pharaohs. I had been face-to-face with God. I had walked the marbled halls in Egypt. I had walked the rocky paths of the wilderness. I had carried the saber of a prince. I had carried the staff of a shepherd. I drank sweet wine from a gold cup. I drank refreshing water from a rock. I was haughty until I was humbled!

Lord, for most of my life, I have been surrounded by thousands, but now I am alone. Alone! *Please come to me in this hour of my heartache…in this shadow of death. I held my brother, Aaron, in my arms when he died. Is there no one here to hold me, no one to comfort me?*

You have been my support and my strength for many years. I could not have led Your people without Your guidance. You gave me fortitude. You blessed me with health. But now, oh, Lord, I am tired, and I feel completely drained! Drained and alone!

Often, I prayed for the lives of Your rebellious children. Who, now, will pray for me? Just say a word of comfort, Lord! A whisper! Once more, please bless me with Your presence. Let me see Your face. Let me hear Your voice. Once more!

My Lord and my God, I can't see You! I can't hear you! Oh, why have You forsaken me? Why have You left me to die alone? Don't You care? Yes, yes, Lord, please forgive me for I know that You care and have not abandoned me! Even though my sin was great, I know that You love me and have forgiven me. Give me peace.

Once more, I put my life…and now my death in Your hands. How much longer, Lord? How long must I wait? How long before peace comes to my mind…and my body? How…long…

M.J. FERGUSON

Moses 120 Years Old

EPILOGUE

A great dark cloud settled over the top of Mount Nebo, indicating to all the Israelites that Moses had died. In their great mourning, they realized that their disobedience and rebellion had provoked their humble leader of forty years to sin against the Great I AM, saying, "*We* are to blame. It is *our* fault."

Although Moses *felt* alone during his last hours on the top of the mountain, he was *not* alone. The God of Israel was there, beside Moses, cradling his head as Moses had done for his brother, Aaron. The lifeless body of Moses was then taken by God to the valley of Moab. He was buried by the angels in a secret place—a place where no one knew. This was done so no man could make a shrine and be in danger of committing idolatry regarding Moses, the great servant of God, as someone to be worshipped.

After a period of lamenting and sincere repentance for thirty days, the dark cloud disappeared, and the unshielded brightness of several angels shone from the top of the mountain. Seeing the brilliant light, the dark mood of the people changed to rejoicing and celebration, saying, "With God and Joshua, we will, at last, be led into the promised land!"

Sometime after the Israelites crossed the Jordan River and entered the promised land of Canaan, the Great I AM, and the angels who buried Moses, came down from Heaven to the humble grave site in the valley of Moab. The Creator of the universe called Moses from his burial chamber and welcomed him into Heaven. Amen.

About the Author

Marilyn J. Ferguson is the author and illustrator of this book. She has written and illustrated 4 other Christian-based books: Eve's Song, The Mirror in the Box, Talon the Raptor, and Their Lives Were Changed.

After Marilyn retired from her nursing career, she had more time to devote to her interest in writing and painting. She has had several shows displaying her artwork. She has also written, directed, and made costumes for 4 Christian-based plays.

Marilyn lives by one of the beautiful Finger Lakes of central NY. She has 2 adult children and 3 grandsons.

CPSIA information can be obtained
at www.ICGtesting.com
Printed in the USA
BVHW010055190721
611810BV00001B/1

9 781638 140009